Valerie Beard
4931 Bethel Rd
Cazenovia, NY 13035

PRAISE FOR
CHANGE YOUR THOUGHTS, CHANGE YOUR WORLD

"The original *Hour of Power* with Robert Schuller Sr. was the very first television ministry to buy time on the then fledgling startup network of TBN in the early seventies. So, needless to say, the Crouch and Schuller families have had a very close and longstanding relationship. However, it's not for this reason that we wholeheartedly endorse Bobby Schuller's book, *Change Your Thoughts, Change Your World*. Living up to his family legacy of encouragement, Bobby does a masterful job empowering his readers and giving them the unique ability to refocus their all-important thought lives. Given the all-out war being waged on hearts and minds these days, we highly recommend this enlightening read for you and your entire family."

—MATT AND LAURIE CROUCH, HOSTS OF
TRINITY BROADCASTING NETWORK

"Bobby has such a gift with words in that he has the rare ability to pack such a fresh vision of truth with such a tender and loving tone just jumping off the page. This book is no exception and it's a must-read! What if we actually believed we could change our thoughts, and then change the world? Well, you can, and Bobby shows us how."

—JEFFERSON BETHKE, *NEW YORK TIMES*
BESTSELLING AUTHOR OF *JESUS > RELIGION*

"The mind is a battlefield of endless thoughts—both positive and negative—that people fight on a daily basis. A constant tug of war where we, as humans, strive to overcome and struggle to hear God's truth in this chaotic culture. Bobby Schuller's book *Change Your Thoughts, Change Your World*, pierces the heart with the beautiful reminder that we should have the mind of Christ. Reading this book gives hope, encouragement, and full armor to those in the midst of this battle, equipping you for a life of peace and freedom."

—DAVID AND ANDREA LOGAN WHITE,
COFOUNDERS OF PURE FLIX ENTERTAINMENT

"Bobby Schuller is a voice of hope in a society looking for it. His ongoing message of God's love is a powerful light in what can seem like a dark world."

—LISA BEVERE, *NEW YORK TIMES* BESTSELLING AUTHOR

"Bobby Schuller will help you change the way you think so you can change your life. He's a friend and encourager that is worth listening to."

—JOHN ORTBERG, PASTOR AND AUTHOR

CHANGE YOUR THOUGHTS, CHANGE YOUR WORLD

How Life-Giving Thoughts
Can Unlock Your Destiny

Bobby Schuller

NELSON
BOOKS

An Imprint of Thomas Nelson

Published in Nashville, Tennessee, by Nelson Books, an imprint of Thomas Nelson. Nelson Books and Thomas Nelson are registered trademarks of HarperCollins Christian Publishing, Inc.

Published in association with Yates & Yates, www.yates2.com.

Thomas Nelson titles may be purchased in bulk for educational, business, fund-raising, or sales promotional use. For information, please e-mail SpecialMarkets@ThomasNelson.com.

Unless otherwise noted, Scripture quotations are taken from the Holy Bible, New International Version®, NIV®. Copyright © 1973, 1978, 1984, 2011 by Biblica, Inc.® Used by permission of Zondervan. All rights reserved worldwide. www.Zondervan.com. The "NIV" and "New International Version" are trademarks registered in the United States Patent and Trademark Office by Biblica, Inc.®

Scripture quotations marked KJV are from the King James Version. Public domain.

Scripture quotations marked THE MESSAGE are from *The Message*. Copyright © by Eugene H. Peterson 1993, 1994, 1995, 1996, 2000, 2001, 2002. Used by permission of NavPress. All rights reserved. Represented by Tyndale House Publishers, Inc.

Any Internet addresses, phone numbers, or company or product information printed in this book are offered as a resource and are not intended in any way to be or to imply an endorsement by Thomas Nelson, nor does Thomas Nelson vouch for the existence, content, or services of these sites, phone numbers, companies, or products beyond the life of this book.

ISBN 978-1-4002-0171-6 (eBook)
ISBN 978-1-4002-0170-9 (HC)
ISBN 978-1-4002-1546-1 (IE)

Library of Congress Control Number: 2018964328

Printed in the United States of America
19 20 21 22 23 LSC 10 9 8 7 6 5 4 3 2 1

To my beloved wife, Hannah, the best thinker I know.

CONTENTS

Contents

INTRODUCTION

Change your thoughts and
you will change the world.
—Norman Vincent Peale

T here is no doubt our thoughts impact our lives. What we think about ultimately results in the decisions that guide our lives. Yet we often don't think about what we think about. We don't realize that our thought lives can be scattered or disciplined, anxious or at peace, filled with faith and hope, or wallowing in despair. Instead, we allow our minds to wander like corks bobbing on the sea. What if we are actually supposed to be training our minds, thinking with discipline, so we can be the people God has called us to be?

This, of course, is what God wants for us. Paul wrote in his letter to the Corinthians to "have the mind of Christ" (1 Cor. 2:16). He told his protégé Timothy, "For the Spirit God gave us does not make us timid, but gives us power, love and self-discipline" (2 Tim. 1:7). Too often, we allow very dark thoughts, like bitterness, entitlement, fear, or despair, to be our norm. Then we self-medicate through substance, work, or other vices to get our minds off of them.

But it doesn't really help in the long run. Jesus said, "When an impure spirit comes out of a person, it goes through arid places seeking rest and does not find it" (Matt. 12:43). That demon leaves, only to come home later to find everything swept and in order. So, he brings seven others to join him!

This is also an analogy of what happens when we try to rid ourselves of dark thoughts without replacing them with new, life-giving thoughts. We just leave a clean, empty house for more bad thoughts to inhabit. There is a better way to control our thoughts, and it's not "try harder."

Learning to control thoughts is the key to a healthy mind. It's important not to allow negative thoughts—jealousy, blame, accusations, or others—to swirl around in our heads. They quickly and easily turn to bitterness and sin. By "thinking about what we think about," we can move from being a person of bitterness to a person of blessing.

Our thoughts need to be trained. To get out of despair and stay out of depression, we must train our minds to focus on whatever is "true . . . noble . . . right . . . pure . . . lovely . . . admirable . . . excellent . . . or praiseworthy," as Philippians 4:8 says.

As a pastor I'm in touch with a lot of pain. I see how often that pain occurs in the mind, in our thinking. People feel isolated, alone, and too depressed to be who they truly want to be. Many of the addictions, relational issues, and shortcomings in our vocation are the result of not training our minds into the right kind of thinking. We all do this.

I've had major struggles in my marriage, my parenting, my business, and my ministry, and I can tell you the solutions I came to only succeeded when I identified the thinking that led to these areas of my life breaking down. Through pain, struggle, research, and experience, I've found a way to have an amazing marriage and family life, to grow my ministry and business, and to live a reasonably happy life most of the time. That's what this book is all about. It begins with training your mind with the Word of God and the thoughts of God.

All of us have both a conscious and an unconscious mind that are working at the same time, all the time. Training has to do with changing not only our conscious mind but our unconscious mind as well. What many refer to as "muscle memory" has very little to do with muscles and everything to do with the mind. Great piano players, for example, will tell you the worst thing they can do when performing a difficult piece is to think about what they are playing. Can you imagine a concert pianist playing Rachmaninoff thinking, *Okay, I need to put this finger here now and press the peddle next?* Whether it's a professional outfielder making an astonishing catch, an ice-skater doing a triple axel, or a kid riding her bike, most of our actions come from training the unconscious part of our minds.

When I was first learning to drive a not-so-mini van as a teenager, I was incredibly nervous. I went through all the things I learned in class. I braked hard, overcorrected the steering, and reminded myself, "The gas is on the right and the brake is on the left." I thought, *How does my big sister drive and do her makeup at the same time? This is hard!*

Of course, after years of driving, most of us don't even think about it consciously anymore. Our driving begins in conscious learning but then goes to a "muscle memory" unconscious place in our minds so we can drive with ease. I'm sure there are many times you've driven several miles in traffic only to suddenly realize you weren't paying attention at all. Your conscious mind was thinking about a meeting you had later in the day, but your unconscious mind was driving the car for you.

In this same way, the unconscious part of our minds is affecting our behavior. When we dwell on negative things, we train our emotional muscle memory, which affects our behavior. But when we learn new life-giving thoughts and train them into our unconscious mind, it affects our work, relationships, investments, and especially our walk with God. This, then, creates a positive feedback loop where the trained mind dwells on new positive thoughts, which create positive outcomes and so on. Over time, this can have a massive positive effect on your life experience.

This book will stress the importance of paying attention to your thought life. That is half the battle. Then it will teach you to train your mind through learning and adopting spiritual disciplines so that you can change your thought life and change your world.

At the beginning of each chapter you'll find a "thought to inherit," which is a new thought that I will explain in detail in the body of the chapter. We'll finish with a short training to help get this thought deeper into your unconscious mind.

This book is not only good for your individual discipleship, but it can also be used within a group setting, such as a small group at church or with another Christian friend. You can exchange your experiences with these various disciplines and discuss whether they were helpful, or even make recommendations to one another on how to improve them.

If you feel stressed out, exhausted, or stuck in a rut and want to live every day with focus, joy, and peace of mind, this book is for you. I want to encourage you to put the training into practice and finish the book. I believe if you put even one of the twelve new thoughts from this book into practice, you will be in a vastly different place five years from now than you would have been without it.

Remember, God loves you just as you are and not as you should be. You don't have to practice any of these disciplines to gain God's love. Rather, this is a gift from his Spirit to yours to help you live in the reality of what you probably believe consciously but perhaps doubt deep in your heart.

This is a guide to a victorious life.

Chapter 1

YOU ARE WHAT YOU THINK ABOUT

As he thinketh in his heart, so is he.

—Proverbs 23:7 KJV

THOUGHT TO INHERIT: *My life is the result of my thinking.*

O nce a man walking through his city came upon a construction site. Curious about what was going on, he asked the first worker laying bricks what he was building. In a bored, slightly irritated voice, he said, "I'm building a wall."

The man kept walking and met another bricklayer and asked the same question. "Oh, I'm building a church," he replied in a relaxed tone. "It will be nice."

Finally, he met a third bricklayer and asked him what he was building. "I'm building a house of God," he said with both joy and conviction. It was the same question, the same job, but three different perspectives.

Who do you suppose was the best worker? Whom would you promote if you were the boss? In describing this colloquial parable, Angela Duckworth says the three men saw their work in three different modes: the first as a job, the second as a vocation, and the third as a calling.[1]

All three men were fostering different thoughts. Ultimately, such thoughts will form three different paths, and instinctively most people want to be on that third path. This man seemed full of joy and purpose, and we assume he worked harder, better, longer, and more energetically than the others. He was happy even though he was doing a job most of us would view as hard labor. Though we know these three men are in the same place in our story, we can assume, all things equal, they would be in very different places five years from now.

You become your thoughts. How you handle the circumstances in your life, whether good or bad, is the result of your thinking. These words are not meant to be a judgment or a criticism but a life-giving revelation. They are meant to give you the hope that, if you can change your thoughts, you can change your whole world. A small change in just one area of thinking in your life can lead to massive changes in your circumstances.

That's good news! The thoughts of today are the results of tomorrow. Your thoughts will always culminate in habit, which influences your circumstances. It is a law woven into the fabric of the universe. In this world, the weakest can become the strongest and the strongest can become the weakest merely by changing the way they think. If the wealthiest, most powerful man in the world loses his wits, he loses everything. Just look to the great king Nebuchadnezzar, who was the most powerful man on earth but lost his mind and, in turn, lost everything.

The Scriptures are true when they say, "As [a man] thinketh in his heart, so is he" (Prov. 23:7 KJV). You are what you think about and what you dwell on. Changing one consistent negative thought into one noble and life-giving thought will alter your life dramatically.

SMALL CHANGES LEAD TO NEW DESTINATIONS

I grew up fishing on the open sea. Every summer of my childhood, from about six years old to seventeen, was spent out on the ocean. I basically lived and worked on a boat, bouncing around the Southern California coast or taking trips to Mexico. The captain sailed the boat from what's called the *fly bridge*, a large tower where he could see kelp, fish, land off in the distance, or anything else of interest. In the fly bridge was a bright, sparkling clean stainless-steel steering wheel.

Everyone assumed this is what he used to steer the ship, but in fact, it was bright and clean because it was never used. Instead, the main tool the captain used to sail the boat was a computer to the left of the wheel with a very small, three-inch plastic dial. This dial was used to alter the course of the ship by a small yet measurable degree you could see on the computer screen. When the captain altered the course by only a couple degrees, no one on the boat would notice or feel it. No one could tell the course had changed. But an hour or two later, those two clicks would have rerouted us so that we ended up far from San Diego. One small turn of the dial over a long period of time leads to massive change.

Small thoughts—like believing in God, forgiving an offender, not blaming authority figures, or being grateful every day—can also make gigantic changes in your life over time, though others may not notice right away.

THE DIFFERENCE IT MAKES

This is what changing your thinking is like. Your thoughts are your destination. The change from an unhealthy thought to a good or godly thought is the difference between heading toward death and heading toward life. The change will be gradual, but in time, everyone will notice you are a very different person. Five years from now your life will be better or worse because of the thoughts you have or have not changed.

Good thoughts always bear good fruit. Bad thoughts always bear bad fruit. You cannot have ugly thoughts and expect to have a beautiful life. You can't have negative thoughts and expect to attract positive people. Good thinking must bear good fruit, and bad thinking must bear thorns and thistles. As Jesus said, "A good tree cannot bear bad fruit, and a bad tree cannot bear good fruit" (Matt. 7:18), so it is with our thinking.

James Allen, pioneer of the self-help movement, said, "Men imagine that thought can be kept secret, but it cannot; it rapidly crystallizes into habit, and habit solidifies into circumstance."[2] He meant that the circumstances of your life are the result of your thinking. People war against the circumstances in their lives while fostering the thoughts that led them there. They hate the effect while loving the cause.

Maybe you are frustrated with your relational life, your progress at work, or your financial outlook. Maybe there's some addiction, sin, or vice in your life you just can't seem to beat. Behind it is a pattern of thinking that led to that result. If you want to change your circumstances and your world, change your thoughts.

Though some circumstances in your life are not directly related to your thinking, your ability to endure adversity will be the result of your thinking. If I have a sick child, for example, it is not because of my wrong thinking, obviously. But my ability to help that child, as well as my ability to be a joyful person, relies solely on how I choose to think during that painful and exhausting trial. Some people will endure immense challenges or tragedies and come out the other side victorious, even joyful, in the midst of loss. Others will come out defeated, exhasuted, depressed, or isolated, even if they won. The difference is how they tended to their thoughts.

PERSPECTIVE

Your spiritual, relational, and financial outlook is directly related to the kinds of thoughts you dwell on. Your ability to press through the challenges of life to real achievement with joy is directly related to your thinking.

When I was sixteen years old, I moved to Tulsa, Oklahoma. I was going through a radical transformation in my spiritual life directly related to training I received on how to think correctly. Much of this training was coming from the sermons and ministry of my new church, Church on the Move, led by Willie George. I couldn't think of a better place for a teenager going through massive change (a new town, new friends, new school, and especially a new, blossoming faith) to be. Pastor George taught me so much about mind-set.

It was during this time in Tulsa that I got my first job. My stepdad arranged it with one of his friends who owned a big Mexican restaurant called Pueblo Viejo. It was there I became an expeditor. Now, on the totem pole of importance at a typical restaurant, you have the general manager and manager at the top, then the bartenders, the servers just under them, then the hostess and busboys, and finally, at the very bottom of the barrel, the expeditor. The technical job of an expeditor is to bring the food out to the table, but at Pueblo Viejo, the actual job was to do all the stuff no one else wanted to do. It was a glory-free scrub position, but I was happy to have it.

One night the restaurant had closed for the evening and we were all ready to go home. I had finished cleaning the kitchen, wiping everything down, and sweeping up nicely. I went the extra mile, and the floor was so clean you could eat off of it. Then, one of the servers brought in some leftover food and dropped the plates down too hard on the counter. A plate full of cheesy rice hit the ground, and food went everywhere. To add insult to injury, the waiter looked at me with a *Well, aren't you going to sweep that up?* kind of look and walked out. That's when my manager walked in, saw the mess, and said, "Schuller! What are you doing? Clean that mess up! I want to go home."

My first response was to be full of rage, to defend myself and point the finger at the guy who made the mess. I loved scrapping with guys like that server, or at least arguing when I felt an injustice had been done. Then I remembered that Pastor George had quoted Martin Luther that week, talking about vocation and honorable work. Luther purportedly said:

> The maid who sweeps her kitchen is doing the will of God just as much as the monk who prays—not because she may sing a Christian hymn as she sweeps but because God loves clean floors. The Christian shoemaker does his Christian duty not by putting little crosses on the shoes, but by making good shoes, because God is interested in good craftsmanship.[3]

In that moment, instead of arguing or blaming, I decided to sweep the floor for God. I decided to let it go. No use arguing. I wasn't doing my work for anyone except the Lord.

Can I tell you that normally this unfair sweeping would have been something I would have huffed about, steaming from the ears? I normally would have tossed and turned that night in smoldering anger, imagining great comebacks I could have said or plotting ways I could get back at that waiter, only to awkwardly avoid eye contact with him next time I saw him. Instead, the sweep became an act of true worship. It actually was joyful, and I went home with a peaceful heart.

In this little moment in my life, I realized the power of good thoughts. On the outside, everything was the same. I did my job and swept the floor. But on the inside, everything was different. One little shift, in a moment that would seem insignificant, could have resulted in days of anger, resentment, and self-pity, which in turn would have likely hurt my job and working relationship with my colleagues. My deleterious thoughts would have had negative, observable consequences. Instead, I received a touch from the Holy Spirit and kept the joy in my little job no one else cared about. This small change had long-term positive consequences in all the jobs and schooling that followed.

DREAM JOBS

How we think about our work can have huge effects, either positively or negatively, not only on our careers but also on every other aspect of our lives. Most people don't like their jobs and daydream about doing something else. But those who are enthusiastic about their work are thriving in their vocations. People think, *He loves his job because he has a great job.* But almost always it's the other way around. He loves his job even when he is doing the thing no one else wants to do. The great job doesn't lead to good thinking. Good thinking leads to the great job.

J. D. Rockefeller is a great example of this. He effectively started with nothing, and at his first job he was paid fifty cents a day to do backbreaking work. Even back then, this was hardly any money. Though most people would have had hard feelings toward an employer who paid so little, Rockefeller celebrated September 26, the day he got his first job, for the rest of his life. He called it "job day."

He also had another good pattern of thought—a deep, unshaking sense of destiny. Rockefeller grew up in a Baptist church and had a sense of calling on his life. He would think about and talk about it regularly. This feeling of destiny was reinforced when one day he was headed to an important meeting. Because of random chance, he missed his train by only a few moments. That train he missed was derailed, killing all on board. Though the experience was traumatic, Rockefeller believed he was spared for a reason.

THE GREAT JOB DOESN'T LEAD TO GOOD THINKING. GOOD THINKING LEADS TO THE GREAT JOB.

Pair these two thoughts—a love of work and a sense of destiny— and you get the life of J. D. Rockefeller, a man who is considered to be the wealthiest person in American history. Of course, money doesn't matter the way the world thinks it does. You certainly can't take it with you, and it is worthless compared to spiritual treasures, but the point remains: we achieve or fail based on how we think. Our thoughts become our reality.

A recent study from the Kellogg School of Management at Northwestern University showed boys typically grow up to make relatively the same amount of money their fathers made. If their dads made $30,000 a year, most likely they will make $30,000 a year. If their dads made $150,000 a year, they most likely will make that amount as adults.[4]

Though many will say "It's their environment" or "They had the privilege of education," I would disagree. I believe the real reason is a pattern of thinking. We look to our parents to see what is considered normal. If Dad makes a little, I can settle for a little. If Dad made six figures, I can't rest until I get there as well. I will have to do what it takes to get there. Here you can see that the thought of expectation, reinforced by the family, leads to grit, which ultimately leads to real financial results.

If you want to change your income, change your thinking. If you want to change your relationships, change your thinking. If you think tomorrow the same way you think today, you will stay more or less where you are.

BUT I CAN'T HELP WHAT I THINK

Maybe you're saying to yourself, *But I can't help what I think about!* Maybe your thoughts and feelings seem to rule you. What then?

Controlling your thoughts is a kind of strength training for the soul. The more weight your mind has to push or pull, the stronger it must be. Though today you may feel incapable of controlling your thinking, I assure you it's possible through training. This is, of course, the way to make any muscle stronger. You must train it. Training is difficult. If it's not difficult, it's not training. But the good news is, though it is difficult today, it will be easier tomorrow because you've already done the hard work.

The Bible refers to such training of the mind as *meditating*. Though this word may sound like the sixties' love for Eastern religion, don't let it scare you. The Bible talks about *meditating* on the Word of God more than it does about *studying* the Word of God, yet so many followers of Jesus are unfamiliar with this notion. The Bible says to "study" the Scripture only four times, while it says to "meditate" on Scripture eighteen times. For example:

"Keep this Book of the Law always on your lips; *meditate* on it day and night, so that you may be careful to do everything written in it. Then you will be prosperous and successful" (Josh. 1:8, emphasis added).

Or the famous opening to the book of Psalms:

Blessed is the one . . . whose delight is in the law of the LORD, and who *meditates* on his law day and night (Ps. 1:1–2, emphasis added).

Rightfully understood, meditating begins with memorizing scriptures that elevate your thinking, and it continues by incorporating those scriptures into your prayer life. In other words, we should not only read and study the Bible; we should *dwell* on it.

Though none of us can control every little thought that comes into our minds, we can control what we dwell on. My wife's grandfather used to say, "You can't keep birds from flying over your head, but you can keep them from making a nest in your hair." When negative thoughts pop into your head about your future, your neighbor, or your life in general, you have the power to dwell on that thought. You also have the power to cast it from your mind and meditate on thoughts that will shape a good life. When you dwell on noble, godly, and beautiful thoughts consistently, you will absolutely be destined for a noble, godly, and beautiful life.

GOOD NEWS

Whatever present circumstance you might dislike or find uncomfortable, there is a way forward—a way out. Change your thinking and you will change your life. Changing your thinking just a little will alter the course of your life dramatically.

The apostle Paul said, "Do not conform to the pattern of this world, but be transformed by the renewing of your mind. Then you will be able to test and approve what God's will is—his good, pleasing and perfect will" (Rom. 12:2). Paul talked a great deal in his letters to the church about changing one's thinking and putting on "the mind of Christ" (1 Cor. 2:16). At the heart of it, if we desire a godly life, we must have a godly mind.

The word here for "transformed" is the Greek word *metamorphosis*. Metamorphosis is a complete and total transformation, where the essence of the thing itself is different. It's what happens when a tadpole becomes a frog, when a caterpillar becomes a butterfly, and when a sinner becomes a saint. It is change at its most radical and extreme. This is transformation that can happen in your life by "renewing your mind." It can happen! If you change your thoughts, you will change your existence.

The thoughts that lead to death are those that conform to the pattern of this world. Those aren't from God. We all need the kinds of thoughts that come from heaven. If we think the way everyone else thinks, we'll get the results everyone else is getting. For an extraordinary life, we need to dwell on extraordinary thoughts.

THE MIND IS A GARDEN

Grandpa Pursley, on my mother's side of the family, had a green thumb. He lived with us when I was a teenager, and I still remember how much he cared for the garden in our backyard. He built a large wooden parameter with a wire fence to keep out little animals. He filled it with topsoil and carefully mapped out where every crop would go. Most of all, he made sure it was always fertilized. He wouldn't let any rotten food or coffee grounds be wasted. They always ended up in the soil. Nearly every day he was out there pulling weeds, making sure the garden was cared for and thriving.

And it did thrive. He had big bright red tomatoes and vegetables of every kind. It was a beautiful thing. When Grandpa Pursley moved to Missouri, his garden no longer got the careful tending he'd been giving it. In less than a month, his garden was completely overrun by weeds.

The same happens with our minds. Your mind is a garden, and it must be kept and cared for. When you plant good ideas, care for them, and protect them, they will yield tremendous good in this life. Good thoughts will lead to good relationships, prosperity, joy, and a general satisfaction with life.

This journey of changing your thoughts should last a lifetime and be the most important thing you do. A disciplined and trained life is a wonderful thing, but if you let it go, the garden of your mind will run wild, and your life will fall apart. You must be vigilant to grow in knowledge, wisdom, and compassion.

YOUR MIND IS A GARDEN, AND IT MUST BE KEPT AND CARED FOR.

Care for your mind as you would a garden. Think about the life you want to have, and dwell on the thoughts that lead to that life. Think like the people you respect, and you will have a life similar to theirs. If you dwell on thoughts of blame, jealousy, judgment, bitterness, self-pity, lust, or pride, the beautiful garden you have made will be choked out. But if you hold on to noble and godly thoughts, like those of worship, forgiveness, compassion, possibility, and "[rejoicing] with those who rejoice" (Rom. 12:15), you will lead a life of victory.

—————————— *Training* ——————————

VERSE TO MEDITATE ON

"Do not conform to the pattern of this world, but be transformed by the renewing of your mind." (Rom. 12:2)

QUESTION TO CONSIDER

What pattern of thinking has led to the most victory or joy in my life?

THOUGHT TO INHERIT

My life is the result of my thinking.

DISCIPLINE TO PRACTICE

The first step in changing your thoughts is to notice them. We rarely think about what we think about. The spiritual discipline of examination is a useful one here.

When you go to bed tonight, sit up in bed, relax your body, and ask the Holy Spirit to speak to you. Fix your mind first on God and nothing else. Then begin to walk through your day, remembering its most important moments, both the highs and the lows. Think about your emotions and label them. Give them to God. Then also remember what you were thinking and feeling when you made decisions that affected your day. How would you have changed them? How will you think differently next time around? Or, if it was a good outcome, how can you think that way more?

By putting the discipline of examination into practice, you will be able to evaluate your life rather than let it merely happen to you.

CHAPTER 2

FROM BLAME TO BLESSING

*I ran my own race. I knew what I
wanted and my perseverance paid off.*

—ROBERT SMITH

THOUGHT TO INHERIT: *God wants me to succeed.*

H ave you ever felt guilty for having a big dream in your heart? Maybe you didn't feel comfortable sharing it because you thought people would roll their eyes or belittle your dream. When we have a vision, goal, or dream, it can be the kind of thing that truly gives us hope. It helps us endure the present sufferings in life, so sharing those dreams with another person feels incredibly vulnerable. But maybe you grew up in a household, religious tradition, or culture that discouraged success as somehow prideful or immoral. You have a drive to succeed, but you try to hide it or feel shame about it.

I remember once observing my mom undergo unfair treatment from a distant cousin. She grew up in a very strict religious community. Most of her family was from the Ozarks in Missouri, and in their religious culture you were expected to play your part. Go to church, get married, have kids, and never be prideful. Anything more than that and you were "too big for yer britches!" She got this message a lot growing up, and she believed that God was mad at her, that she wasn't lovable, and that she should keep her head down and always follow the rules.

When I was a kid, my family traveled from our home in Los Angeles to a massive family reunion in a small town in Oklahoma I'd never heard of. Fifty or so of our distant relatives had gathered, and we had great food, great music, and lots of love and laughter. Honestly, it was wonderful. That's why I was so surprised when a bizarre exchange happened. At the dinner table, my mom shared that she was working on a novel with some colleagues, a dream she'd carried in her heart for a long time. She had a warm smile on her face as she walked her family through the narrative of her story. Out of nowhere, a relative condescendingly dismissed my mom: "Oh Linda, you're just a dreamer!" In her family, living in Los Angeles and writing a novel was "too big for yer britches."

I was just a young kid, but I remember being so angry with that woman. Years later, when I mentioned it to my mom, she remembered the story vividly and told me that after, she heard those words play like a loop in her mind through the whole project: "Oh Linda, you're just a dreamer." The project was never finished, and my mom wondered aloud if that tape playing over and over in her mind had something to do with it. Did she ultimately believe those words? "People have no idea the power their words have on others," she said to me over the phone.

Maybe you have similar words going through your head. Maybe those words came from a person you truly love and respect. You wonder, *Maybe they're right. Maybe I'm just a dreamer. Maybe I'm being prideful.* Let go of that! Be free. God loves dreamers like Joseph, David, Mary, and the apostle Paul. He loves dreamers like you. Though our goals and dreams change, and certainly some goals and dreams should be abandoned, never believe the lie that somehow success is prideful. Very often the enemy wants you to believe that because he's afraid of the good you'll do if you succeed.

LET GO OF GUILT

Never be ashamed of desiring more from your life. Never feel bad about wanting to achieve great things or to be happy. Jesus teaches us how we should live and think, and as long as we abide by those teachings (generosity, honesty, and compassion, for example), we should strive for success in every area of our lives. For some this means financial success, for others it's a widely influential ministry, and for still others it's raising wonderful children. No matter what, never feel guilty for having a big dream in your heart. God very likely put it there, and if he did, you have a responsibility to pursue it. You can absolutely feel great about that.

Try your best not to feel guilty for wanting more from life. The real trap of the devil is when we settle for ordinary when we've been given what we need to do great things.

Success is your responsibility, your moral mandate. If God calls you to do something, don't abandon that call. Keep pressing on. Failure in and of itself is not a sin because we must go through many failures to grow and ultimately reach our goals. For every one of our successes in life, we may experience ten failures first. The sin is in giving up entirely, walking away from God's calling because you are tired, angry, or have lost heart. You can look to stories like Jonah's or the parable of the talents for evidence of this.

> IF GOD CALLS YOU TO DO SOMETHING, DON'T ABANDON THAT CALL.

Abandon the hidden shame you may feel about your desire to succeed. Many pastors and Christian teachers have confused the concepts of success and calling with those of narcissism, pride, and inflated egos. They suggest you can't be successful, achieving great things, and still be a humble servant living totally in God's will. In this way, many Christian leaders are complicit in their followers' sin of sloth. Though many people take pride in what they have, others have pride in what they don't have, and the devil is loving it. Be free from the idea that somehow you have to feel guilty for succeeding, and remind yourself, *Success is my responsibility, a moral mandate.*

TALENTS

Don't equate success with finances. That perspective is far too narrow. Rather, success is achieving the big purposes and callings you have in your life from God. Succeeding means pushing through the pain, challenges, and setbacks in life. We can succeed in marriage, work, ministry, and anything else the Spirit of God calls us to if we take on the mantle of Jesus and carry on his work in the world.

The word *success* is from the Latin *successus*, which means "an advance, a coming up." It doesn't mean just achieving, but achieving after someone else; in our case, we succeed after Christ and our mentors. *Success* literally means "to take on the mantle of Christ and keep doing what he did." You hear it more clearly in the word *succession*. It's as though Christ is holding out the baton to you. Will you take it?

Jesus was passionate about his disciples doing greater things than he and using their gifts and talents to achieve great things for the kingdom of God. He was very serious about this and even used heavy language to describe those who wasted their talents. In his famous parable of the talents, Jesus said a master left for a long time and put his wealth under the management of three servants. To the first servant, he gave five talents (a measurement of gold). To the second he gave two talents, and to the third he gave one. When the master returned, the one who was given five talents had made five more:

His master replied, "Well done, good and faithful servant! You have been faithful with a few things; I will put you in charge of many things. Come and share your master's happiness!" (Matt. 25:21)

The second servant also doubled his talents, and the master gave the same elated reply:

"Well done, good and faithful servant! You have been faithful with a few things; I will put you in charge of many things. Come and share your master's happiness!" (25:23)

But the third had buried the talent because he was so afraid of losing it. He simply gave the one talent back to the master.

His master replied, "You wicked, lazy servant! So you knew that I harvest where I have not sown and gather where I have not scattered seed? Well then, you should have put my money on deposit with the bankers, so that when I returned I would have received it back with interest.

"So take the bag of gold from him and give it to the one who has ten bags. For whoever has will be given more, and they will have an abundance. Whoever does not have, even what they have will be taken from them." (25:26–29)

Jesus was not giving this message to a crowd of listeners. He was speaking privately to his twelve disciples. He was saying, "I have given you knowledge, the Holy Spirit, and a certain number of talents. I am now going to my Father. It's your time to succeed me. I command it." Success is not for you; it's for the Lord. God's given you everything you need to achieve what you were called to do.

Stop thinking these sorts of things:

I will succeed someday . . .
I can't succeed because I am too (fill in the blank)
I can't succeed because I am not (fill in the blank) enough.

Think instead: *Success is my responsibility.*

The Bible says, "For as he thinketh in his heart, so is he" (Prov. 23:7 KJV). This is true of nearly every aspect of your life, including your achievements. Though things like luck, a fair and just working environment, and a good starting hand all help, in the end, the most successful people are those who have the right kind of thinking even when those advantages are not in place. Some of the most successful people in the world are so because they endured times of terrible luck and didn't give up. They were dealt terrible hands, like being abandoned by their parents, growing up in poverty, or suffering abuse in some way. Despite those things, they accomplished a great deal. In the end, life will not be fair all the time to any of us, and when we get down on our luck we need to foster the kind of thoughts that will get us to where we dream of being.

You have more power over your thoughts than you do over your achievements. In other words, your thoughts are perfectly designed to give you the results you're getting out of your life. James Allen said, "All that a man achieves and all that he fails to achieve is the direct result of his own thoughts."[1]

People who think carefully about their goals, write them down, and prioritize them will achieve more than people who merely dream when they feel bored with life. Dr. Gail Matthews did an extensive study of individuals who wrote down their goals versus those who didn't and found that "you become 42 percent more likely to achieve your goals and dreams, simply by writing them down on a regular basis."[2] Also, people who understand that succeeding at one goal often means failing at another will achieve more. People who look to others to get feedback on their plans will achieve more. People who believe in their plans and in their goals, even when things are rocky and they don't know if they will make it through—they, too, will achieve a great deal. And those who foster the right kinds of thoughts by learning, reading, and seeking out mentors will achieve more.

Achievement is not the result of luck. Achievement is not the result of being brought up in the right environment. Achievement is not the result of fairness. I have never heard a great achiever say, "I accomplished my dreams and goals because I was in a fair environment." You can do this. Believe it, and you will achieve it.

OWN YOUR LIFE

Great achievers don't blame their parents, their colleagues, God, or their environment. Instead, they take as much responsibility for their lives as they reasonably can. They decide that if their lives are ever going to change, it's going to start with them. It's the kind of thinking that says, *Despite the pain, the unfairness, or the setback, I will get better, learn more, and change the plan so that it will create better results.* Achievers are lifelong learners committed to never giving up on growing. They relish feedback and criticism, and they are transparent because they care more about getting better than they do about looking good.

These are also the thoughts we ought to have if we are going to achieve great things for God. The thoughts that lead to success are the thoughts that are taught throughout the Bible, especially Proverbs. Jesus taught us that we would do greater things than even he did, because he was going to his Father. If I'm called to achieve greater things than Jesus, it's prudent for me to learn how to do that.

God will do great things in your life. Don't disqualify yourself in your thinking. Don't say to yourself:

- "I'M TOO TIRED. THIS SOUNDS EXHAUSTING." It's not! Though it's hard work, long-term success is one of the most energy-building and life-giving things you can do.
- "I'M TOO UNEDUCATED OR INEXPERIENCED." There's never been greater access to information, education, mentors, and internships than there is today. *Doing* is the way most people learn, so get started.
- "I'M TOO OLD." When a ninety-nine-year-old woman received her diploma, she advised prospective students, "Don't give up. Do it. Don't let anybody discourage you. Say that, 'I'm going to do it,' and do it for yourself."[3]
- "I'M TOO YOUNG." One of the best ways to grow is through failure. Start failing now so you can succeed later.
- "I'M TOO MUCH OF A SINNER/DOUBTER." God loves to use imperfect people to do impossible things. Think of all the great heroes of the Bible. They were all messed up and had baggage. I find that people who decide to do great things for God even though they don't have it all together often find the solution they were looking for by simply being in God's calling. Or, as it's been famously said, "God doesn't call the qualified. He

qualifies the called." God will make you holy as you pursue his dreams for your life.

WHAT'S GETTING IN THE WAY OF YOUR SUCCESS?

The greatest enemy to achievement is blame.

It's not unfairness.

It's not bad luck.

It's not lack of money.

It's blame.

Blame is doubly harmful because first it poisons our hearts and leads to sin and further separation from the people we love. But second, it gives us a license not to achieve. It's a way to bow out of our dreams and goals because the pain and sacrifice it takes to get where we are supposed to go is too daunting. Hard work is not the only pain that lies between us and our destiny. It's also the pain of betrayal, partnerships that go awry, and other unforeseen negative circumstances. When pain occurs, the temptation is to blame others because that allows us to get out without feeling the shame of quitting. Make no mistake: the day you begin to blame others is the day you begin to quit.

Failure can lead to either reflection (growth) or blame (death). If we blame others when we fail, we have already taken a major step toward ultimate failure: not only failure of the dream or task at hand but in life in general. People who blame are people who fail. That's not who you are or who you want to be. Forgive those who have hurt you, messed up your plans, or treated you unfairly. Get free in your thought life and chart a new path to successful living.

GENESIS BLAME GAME

Blame is a fundamental part of the cycle of sin and shame in the world. Look at the origin story of Adam and Eve. After Adam and Eve ate from the Tree of Knowledge of Good and Evil, they covered their nakedness (an ancient way of saying they were incredibly ashamed), and they blamed each other. Because they were ashamed, they desperately reached for a solution to escape the pain and shame of failure.

Looking at Adam and Eve is like looking in a mirror. Rarely is any one person totally responsible for a major mistake or blunder. There's usually a backstory, previous hurts, emotions, and inflated egos. Because of that, it's so much easier to blame others than to face the reality of the following:

- I failed.
- I messed up.
- I need to take responsibility for this.

And, of course, the next thing we learn from Adam and Eve is that this ego-driven blame game only drives our children, friends, and society into further isolation. It keeps us wallowing in anger and self-pity rather than causing us to look at ourselves honestly, evaluate, and improve. We fail to take the opportunity to understand that "I'm human; I made a mistake," and instead say, "It was her fault."

Be the bigger person and do your best to take responsibility for your mistakes. No one is perfect, but being responsible is a great way to grow and earn trust from the people who love you.

Blame is the greatest enemy to the thinking that leads to

achieving great things for God. Blame will give you the card you need to quit and not feel shame. Blame is a drug, and most people are addicts. If you want to succeed, you have to think differently.

OWN IT

When things fall apart, it's usually good to take as much blame as possible and dish out as little blame as possible. When I say, "Take the blame," I don't mean that you need to feel ashamed or beat yourself up. That also leads to failure. Rather, I mean owning your part. You can choose to objectively and rationally say, "I messed up. I take responsibility. I'm going to reflect and find new plans and principles to help me achieve in the future." When that happens, you grow.

Owning your responsibility is authentic and relational. In a nonshameful way, it says, "Hey colleagues, family, and friends, I messed up or failed. What's my blind spot? How can I get better?" Though their feedback will not always be right, this kind of transparency will help you get insight into seeing your actions and decisions more objectively. That, too, will foster the thoughts that lead to achievement.

Don't indulge friends if they say, "You don't have any blind spots." They are just afraid of offending you, a greater sign your ego may be bigger than you realize. Resolving to always learn, improve, and think "success is my responsibility and no one else's" will lead to a successful life.

I will make you a promise: If you are looking for someone or something to blame, you will always find it. Nothing will ever be fair in your life. You will always have enemies. In fact, the more you achieve, the less fair life will be and the more enemies you will have. If you can't handle unfairness and enemies, you can't handle success. In this way, enemies are good for you because they reveal and exploit your weaknesses. If you're smart, you'll learn from them and grow.

I love stories of achievement and overcoming. In fact, I've become a student of them. Take a moment and think of some of the famous people you admire. It's likely they've had a life just as hard (or harder) than yours. They'll tell you that the challenges they faced made them better, stronger, and smarter. What if the challenges of your life are even now making you better, stronger, and smarter?

IF YOU CAN'T HANDLE UNFAIRNESS AND ENEMIES, YOU CAN'T HANDLE SUCCESS.

YOUR FINANCES WON'T STOP YOU FROM SUCCEEDING. Billionaire author J. K. Rowling submitted her first draft of *Harry Potter and the Philosopher's Stone* on yellow legal pads. She couldn't afford a typewriter! She is now wealthier than the Queen of England.

ILLNESS WON'T STOP YOU FROM SUCCEEDING. Stephen Hawking, who suffered from ALS, had only the strength to move his cheek muscle. He used that one cheek muscle to speak through a computer. He used it to move his wheelchair around. And he used that little muscle, in fact, to write several books on physics that have changed the world.

PREJUDICE WON'T STOP YOU FROM SUCCEEDING. Robert Smith, America's wealthiest African American, was a baby when his mom took him to the March on Washington where Dr. Martin Luther King Jr. gave his "I Have a Dream" speech at the National Mall in Washington, DC. Despite facing racism periodically in life, Robert Smith went on to be a tremendous success.

As an adult he would apply for his dream job at Bell Technologies even though he didn't have the prestigious degrees or privilege of the others applying for the same job. He didn't get the job. It was the seventies, and he could have assumed they didn't hire him because of his skin color. He may have been right. But instead, he chose not to think those thoughts. Rather, he persisted. He called every day for two weeks, then every Monday for five months, letting them know that if anything changed, he was the man for the job. Every single day for weeks he called. One day, the man who originally got the job didn't show up to work. Guess who they called to fill the role? Robert Smith. That one job led to Smith becoming an engineer, and eventually he became a global force for tech mergers, ultimately leading to his success as a multibillionaire leader in the market.

A reporter recently asked Smith, "What was the key to your success?" He simply said, "I knew what I wanted and my perseverance paid off." Now, the interesting thing is, he didn't mention his own ethnicity until the subject of Barack Obama came up. It just didn't seem like a factor for Smith. He recalled attending Obama's first inauguration with his ninety-three-year-old grandfather who was a coat clerk at the US Senate. Were they surprised that Obama made it to the White House? Before I get to Smith's answer, let me digress for a moment.

I was in seminary when then senator Barack Obama was running for president, and I was taking a course on black history, led by a brilliant African American professor. She had been through a lot in her life, and we as a class could tell she wrestled with feelings of anger because of the racism she'd endured. I asked her, "Do you think Senator Obama will win?" She said, "Absolutely not. America is just too racist to elect a black president."

I'm sure many black Americans agreed with her—but not Robert Smith. He said he was not surprised when Barack Obama won. "We are only bound by the limits of our own conviction,"[4] he said. That is the kind of thinking that leads to victory. Those are the kinds of thoughts that will get you where few other people can get. To achieve what no one else has achieved, you have to dwell on the things no one thinks about and cast out the rubbish everyone else dwells on.

THE BIG LIE

The biggest lie is that success is all on *you*. It's not. God is on your side. If God's on your side, you can accomplish anything you put your mind to. Nothing will stop you if you trust in him and keep the right kind of thinking in place. You are not "too" anything to thrive and triumph.

One of my favorite people in the world is my dear friend Nick Vujicic. Nick was born with no arms and no legs. He is only in his thirties, but he has a beautiful wife and children and has preached the gospel to over 600 million people around the world. He said to me once, "In some ways I'm thankful for my plight because the way I look opens the door for people to listen to what I have to say."[5] When he was a child, he didn't want that kind of attention. But now he is thankful for it! His lack of arms and legs feeds his preaching in a way that elevates it to higher standards.

There will always be bullies, misogynists, bigots, and racists. In turn, there will always be a victor who rises above them and says, "I don't care. I'm going to do what I'm called to do." Nothing will stop you from achieving what God has called you to do except wrong thinking. All that a person achieves or fails to achieve is the result of his or her thinking.

> Learn.
> Evaluate.
> Plan.
> Dream.
> Get back up after a fall.
> Press through the pain.

God believes in you and has called you. If you are alive, it's because God still has a purpose for your life. Pursue that purpose with all your heart. No one is going to succeed for you. It's your calling, your responsibility, and your gift.

BACKSTORY BEHIND THE BLESSING

What do we do when life is totally unfair and the results of where we are are completely out of our control? One of the most commonly cited verses in the Bible is Jeremiah 29:11:

> "For I know the plans I have for you," declares the LORD, "plans
> to prosper you and not to harm you, plans to give you hope and
> a future."

I love this verse. It's pretty popular, frankly. I'm convinced this is the most tattooed Bible verse in the world. It's one that echoes for everyone when they wonder, *Will I ever get out of this?* or *Does God really have a plan for my life?* It's hard to believe it when we go through so much, when we've been rejected so many times, or when we've failed over and over. Yet God says it:

I
have
a
plan
for
you,
and
it's
good.

What's so surprising and delightful in this verse is that, in this passage, God is speaking to a people who

- had sinned,
- felt abandoned by God,
- and were under judgment.

See, this part of Jeremiah was written to the Jews in captivity in Babylon.

They'd been taken from their homes in chains and sent almost a thousand miles away from Israel, a journey that would have taken about four months. They'd been separated from their families and friends and were suffering terribly. Here's what God said to them in Jeremiah 29:

This is what the LORD Almighty, the God of Israel, says to all those I carried into exile from Jerusalem to Babylon: "Build houses and settle down; plant gardens and eat what they produce. Marry and have sons and daughters; find wives for your sons and give your daughters in marriage, so that they too may have sons and daughters. Increase in number there; do not decrease. Also, seek the peace and prosperity of the city to which I have carried you into exile. Pray to the LORD for it, because if it prospers, you too will prosper." (vv. 4–7)

Then later in the chapter:

This is what the LORD says: "When seventy years are completed for Babylon, I will come to you and fulfill my good promise to bring you back to this place. For I know the plans I have for you," declares the LORD, "plans to prosper you and not to harm you, plans to give you hope and a future." (vv. 10–11)

There are three things that stick out to me when I read this— three power thoughts that can dramatically change your experience and outcomes in life:

- Bloom where you're planted.
- Bless your captors.
- You will not be in this hard place forever.

First, many of the Jews in captivity were feeling guilty because they were under judgment from God for their idolatry and for being cruel to the poor. They may have thought they would never be happy again and would never go home again, but it's almost as though God said, "Okay, now I want you to be blessed in a new way."

He told them to build homes, plant gardens, and flourish. He said, I want you to grow and thrive even though you are in captivity. In a way, he says this to all of us when we are caught in a situation we can't get out of. Sometimes God wants us to bloom right where we are planted. This is so we can be the kinds of people we are supposed to become to inherit our destiny, our Israel, in the next good chapter of our lives.

It reminds me of one of my favorite thinkers and writers, Viktor Frankl. He suffered through the concentration camps of Nazi Germany, and through it all, he strove to find meaning even within the unjust suffering he faced. Though he lost his family and friends, who were murdered at the hands of the Nazis, he refused to allow poison to enter his heart. It was there he learned so many of the lessons that led to him writing the legendary work *Man's Search for Meaning*. One of his famous quotes, which applies to everyone, is "When we are no longer able to change a situation . . . we are challenged to change ourselves."[6] This thought is radical and awesome. The idea is to come to terms with an unchangeable present and, in turn, change yourself in a positive way. I write more on this powerful shift in chapter 9.

Next, God challenged the Israelites to bless the Babylonians. Notice, he didn't say, "Throw Molotov cocktails, fight for your land, and declare war." Rather, he said, "Seek the peace and prosperity of the city to which I have carried you into exile," because when the city was blessed, they would be blessed too. Jesus later taught his disciples something even more radical—love your enemies. This isn't just about action. It's about thoughts and intent. So often, when we feel we are treated unfairly, our response is to curse, hate, and blame those who have harmed us. Instead, it's better *for us* to move on and be a blessing to everyone. Doing so will open doors for us and help us lead happier lives.

Finally, he told them, "You will not be here forever." Everyone has been unhappy at some point. Everyone has faced superlow times in life. But the worst thing that happens in those low times are thoughts like:

- *I will be here forever.*
- *I'll never get out.*
- *It will always be the same.*

These nagging thoughts drive many people to extremes like suicide. They think, "I'll always be depressed," or "I'll always have this illness; I can't even remember what it's like to feel healthy." But the good news is, God really does have a plan. Things really will be okay, but you must not give up, not do something irrational or extreme. Things won't always be bad. The you of tomorrow will thank the you of today for keeping hope alive.

The great thing about life is it's always changing, even when we don't want it to. I promise, you will not be stuck in your bad place forever. When you don't give up, that gives God the time he needs to bring you to where you are called to be. There is nothing worse than thinking:

- *I'll always be single and I don't want to be.*
- *I'll always be poor.*
- *I'll always be unemployed.*
- *I'll always doubt God.*

Everyone has felt this way. You are not alone. God promises you that he has plans to prosper you and that he will get you to your destiny. Don't throw away your tomorrow.

You are going to achieve great things with your life, but to do that you will need to foster the kinds of thoughts that will get you there. Don't blame others; instead, always be growing and improving. Dream, plan, press through, and get feedback from your peers. If you do this, there is no limit to what you will accomplish with your life. Success is your responsibility. It's a moral mandate to succeed at what God has called you to do (Matt. 25:14–30). Dwell on this idea and your world will change.

--- *Training* ---

VERSE TO MEDITATE ON

"Very truly I tell you, whoever believes in me will do the works I have been doing, and they will do even greater things than these, because I am going to the Father." (John 14:12)

QUESTION TO CONSIDER

Who is someone I could blame less and bless more?

THOUGHT TO INHERIT

God wants me to succeed.

DISCIPLINE TO PRACTICE

Loving your enemies is a central teaching to the Christian faith. It's right in the heart of Jesus' message. This difficult practice is practical in two dimensions: it benefits *them* and it benefits *you*, because you cease to ingest the poison of bitterness.

Pray a blessing for your enemies for three days. Ask that God would help them, would bring them around to see the way they hurt you and others, and even boldly pray that they would come to know God and be blessed.

Perhaps you say, "I don't have any enemies." In the modern world, this is common. Dallas Willard would instruct you to pray for your competitors.[7] Think about the people in your life you feel competitive toward or who have a competitive posture toward you. Pray that God would bless them and do well in them. Watch how this practice from Jesus will not only eliminate some pain you may be experiencing in your soul but also train you to remove blame from your thinking.

CHAPTER 3

YOU ARE FAVORED.
YOU HAVE A DESTINY.

*Faith is . . . a living, daring
confidence in God's grace, so sure
and certain that a man would stake
his life on it a thousand times.*

—MARTIN LUTHER

THOUGHT TO INHERIT: *God favors me. Good things are coming.*

In high school, my small group of friends and I would often play basketball after school. We all had nicknames, and one of the kids we called "Wall Street," because on his birthday his dad bought him five shares of Nike stock. We would tell girls he "owned Nike," which was technically true. He was the only kid any of us knew who owned stock. He didn't know anything about business, and he didn't even seem interested in it, frankly. His dad probably picked Nike stock because his son liked basketball, but the name stuck, and now I can't even remember what his real name was.

In the end, what do you think Wall Street did for a living? He became an investment banker. People spoke that name over him so much—"Wall Street, Wall Street"—that it became a part of how he viewed himself. When people heard of the actual Wall Street, they thought of him. Wall Street literally became a part of his identity, so much so that even his close friends, like me, forgot his real name. When the time came to pick a career path, the identity he'd been given through that nickname manifested into a life path.

What you see in life, in people, and in your future will become reality. It's the principle of faith. When you see something that is not yet a reality, you are essentially releasing your faith into it. This starts in our thinking and culminates in our speech. First, we think it, then we say it, and then it happens.

If you see the best in your future, you'll get the best. If you see the worst, you'll get the worst. If you see the worst in your colleagues, friends, or family, they will give you their worst. You may have catlike Jedi reflexes, but if someone calls you clumsy and you believe it, you will become clumsier. Or imagine someone who is known by everyone to be rude or inconsiderate. Imagine this person uncharacteristically opens the door for someone else and you say to him, "Chip, that was so polite. You are such a polite person. Thank you." Watch as Chip starts opening doors for people and becomes more hospitable.

What we see in others and what we see in ourselves become our reality. When it stays in our thinking long enough, when we dwell on it, it becomes true. This is why we must become believers in the promises of God. We must believe in favor and destiny, even when things are not going well.

Because the mind is a garden, tending to good, noble thoughts will lead to a good and noble life. But not tending to your thoughts will lead to a garden full of weeds—wild, overgrown, and unfruitful. This is because base, ignoble thoughts are the most natural thoughts of all, the kinds that come when we stop paying attention or working hard at our thought life. Good, fruitful, positive, and purposeful thinking is difficult.

Your thoughts become *you*. I'm not talking about the fleeting thoughts that pop in and out of your head. I'm talking about what you dwell on; those thoughts become your destiny. If you have bitter thoughts, you will become a bitter person. If you have thoughts of peace, you will become a peaceful person. In short, what you dwell on begins to show in your circumstances, so dwell on the kinds of things that will shape the life you want to have.

It's easy to have good thoughts when things are going well—when you're making money, when you're healthy, when your kids are doing well, or when something "lucky" just happened to you. But in the hard times, optimistic thinking becomes simultaneously the most difficult and the most crucial. During these times we rarely feel like believing in a better future or looking for a way forward. When we are out of energy, it's hard to get out of bed and get on with the day. But staying hopeful and positive when circumstances are not going the way you hoped or planned is one of the best things you can do to make sure you get through whatever it is you're going through.

DWELL ON THE LIGHT

The best way to stay hopeful and positive is to understand the promises of God. You really do have a great calling. You really are going to get through your trials to something better. You are a beloved "unceasing spiritual being with an eternal destiny in God's great universe,"[1] as Dallas Willard put it. Thinking about your good destiny, meditating on God's love and goodwill toward you, and believing in favor will make all the difference in enduring the hardships of life. You are not alone in your suffering.

It's not merely what you see in life that becomes your destiny, *it's what you focus on.* By no means do I think when you go through tough times, you just "stay positive" and pretend everything is okay. Rather, believing in favor means thinking, *This is really hard. I'm very sad about this. But God is good, and he has a great purpose for me. This setback won't ruin me!* That kind of thinking and self-talk will make all the difference. I'm not recommending that you pretend the darkness isn't there. I'm simply asking you not to dwell on it and instead dwell on the light.

It's like this: Once there were two artists painting the landscape of Los Angeles. They were both looking at the same city from the same vantage point at the same time of day, painting side by side. The first landscape painting made LA look run down. There was graffiti, barbed wire, and it looked dangerous and unwelcoming. This was not a city you'd want to visit; it was ominous and dark.

The second painting was quite the opposite. It was beautiful. You noticed the architecture, the palm trees, and the sunlight. This was a romanticized LA, the kind people want to see when they migrate from the Midwest. It was a warm, happy place where you could chase after your dreams.

So which painting was real? Well, they both were. Looking at the painting, and then looking up at the skyline, you would see that each artist was portraying Los Angeles. You would see the world through the artists' eyes. Both were real, both had aspects of light and dark. The difference was focus. The positive painting wasn't less real, and it didn't ignore the bad stuff. It merely didn't highlight it.

There will always be dark and light, good and bad in your life. See both, acknowledge both, grieve the bad, but focus and believe in the good. What you focus on you'll believe in, and what you believe in will become your reality. What you see will become your existence.

LUCK

In July 1995 the *New York Times* published an article about an Israeli woman named Anat Ben-Tov. She was lying in a hospital because she had just survived her second bus bombing. She was the lone survivor in an earlier attack that killed twenty-two people. Since then she had an ominous feeling she was "living on borrowed time." Not long after, bus no. 5 exploded, injuring thirty-five and killing six, including the bomber. Lying there in the hospital, the thirty-five-year-old secretary said, "I have no luck, or I have all the luck. I'm not sure which it is."[2]

An article published by *Nautilus* claims that this intriguing story led a researcher at the University of Oslo, Karl Halvor Teigen, and later many other economists and psychologists, to study luck as a science.[3] Were people really lucky or unlucky? Did their perceptions affect their outcomes?

One of those researchers, Richard Wiseman, believes that luck is, in a way, made real by simply believing in it. When you believe you are a lucky person, things seem to just go better in your life. "It turns out believing you are lucky is a kind of magical thinking. . . . A belief in luck can lead to a virtuous cycle of thought and action."[4] Believing you are lucky gives you a greater sense of control in life. This, in turn, leads to a higher sense of optimism, that you are the master of your destiny. Wiseman also shows that people who believe they are lucky have a much lower rate of anxiety, which in turn has its own significant benefits.

When you bring this sense of control, optimism, and low anxiety into a job interview or a first date, you tend to do much better than you would if you felt anxious or worried that everything would go wrong. Because of this, the outcomes created by believing you are lucky create a positive feedback loop. This loop reinforces your circumstances, and you do, indeed, have a lucky life. In other words, believing you are lucky makes it so.

One study Wiseman conducted had to do with finding pictures in a newspaper. He broke the test subjects into two groups, those who believed they were lucky and those who didn't. He gave them each a newspaper and asked them to count how many pictures were in the newspaper and report their best answer. The catch was, on the second page of every newspaper he put the correct answer: "There are thirty-two pictures in this newspaper." He found that most of those who considered themselves lucky found this cheat sheet right away, while those who didn't think of themselves as lucky tended to miss it.[5]

There's something that happens to the vision of people who think of themselves as lucky. Because they think they are leading a lucky life, they look for lucky circumstances, and because of that they are more likely to find them. The innate desire to search for opportunity is something that others lack, so when opportunity really does arise, they are likely to be the first to see it.

WHAT YOU SEE IS WHAT YOU GET

While people who think they are lucky are more likely to see opportunity, people who think they are unlucky are more likely to miss opportunities. A researcher and psychologist at the University of Leicester, John Matby, said, "People who believe in bad luck don't engage in some of the processes needed to bring about positive outcomes."[6]

This idea was reinforced in the Lucky Parkers study. Do you know the kind of person who brags about always finding the best parking spot, the one right up front? This study showed that this braggadocio is usually right. Apparently, people who consider themselves lucky are actually more likely to find a good parking spot. This isn't because of real luck, but rather, they drive directly to the front of the lot. They look slowly for the spot. They are less likely to move on when a spot hasn't appeared, and finally, when it does, they turn on their blinker to claim it. Conversely, those who think themselves unlucky, and therefore less likely to get a spot, may take a quick glance then move on and settle for their typical unlucky parking spot.

WHILE PEOPLE WHO THINK THEY ARE LUCKY ARE MORE LIKELY TO SEE OPPORTUNITY, PEOPLE WHO THINK THEY ARE UNLUCKY ARE MORE LIKELY TO MISS OPPORTUNITIES.

These studies show clearly that what we look for in our lives becomes true. If you think you are lucky, you will have lucky outcomes. If you think you are unlucky, you will have unlucky outcomes in your life. Of course, luck isn't a real thing, but believing in it makes it real because of what is happening in your thoughts.

The great weakness for people who believe themselves lucky is, once they get a bad string of hard luck, they may find themselves now thinking that they are unlucky. The same kind of thinking that originally helped them begins hurting them. But what if in our thinking, regardless if things were good or bad, we simply believed they would ultimately be good no matter what? What if, instead of thinking in terms of random chance from a chaotic universe, we believed in something real—favor and blessing?

BETTER THAN LUCK

This is what Christians believe in—not good luck, but favor. Favor is the idea that, despite what's happened so far, things will ultimately work out for my good. Favor says, "Despite the fact I've messed up a few times along the way, the cross is good enough. God isn't going to punish me. He's cheering me on." God is good, and he truly does bless us. He gives us hope, which produces faith (or, the right kind of thinking), and faith produces results.

The apostle Paul was an amazing man who lived an amazing life, but he really went through a lot. Tradition says that Paul was likely a man small in stature.[7] This wasn't helped by the fact that the name Paul means "short one." Though he preached quite a bit, people seemed to think his sermons were boring. They would much prefer to listen to great orators like Apollos. Once when Paul was preaching, he was so boring that a guy sitting in the third-story window dozed off and fell back out of the window, dying on impact. Paul went down and raised him from the dead and continued preaching his "boring" sermon (Acts 20:7–12).

Paul survived a shipwreck. He was beaten, often imprisoned. Once an angry mob stoned him because they didn't like what he was saying; they didn't want to hear the gospel. Thinking he was dead, they walked away. After lying unconscious for a few hours, resilient Paul got back up and started preaching again.

YOU ARE CALLED

In his famous letter to the Romans, the suffering servant Paul encouraged believers, reminding them that they have a destiny in God's good universe. He said, "And those he predestined, he also called; those he called, he also justified; those he justified, he also glorified" (Rom. 8:30). It's like this:

Destiny → Calling → Justification → Glorification

A pre-destiny means that, before you were born, God chose you. Because of this, even when you were broken and messing up, he called you to do something amazing in his kingdom. Even in the midst of your sin, he said, "I have something good in store for you!" To prepare you for this calling, he justified you, meaning he removed all your sin and shame through Jesus' good work on the cross. And finally, he will glorify you. He will get you to your destiny. You will cross the finish line.

GOD IS NOT SURPRISED BY YOUR MISTAKES. HE HASN'T CHANGED HIS MIND ABOUT YOU BECAUSE YOU'VE MESSED UP.

God is not surprised by your mistakes. He hasn't changed his mind about you because you've messed up. He loves you and wants to do great things in your life. Believe it. Belief isn't just consenting to a truth. Belief changes the way you think, see, and speak. This, in turn, changes your actions. Believe in your destiny so you can inherit it. No mistake, blunder, evil person, sickness, policy, or anything else can keep you from where you are supposed to go. That's why Paul continued:

> No, in all these things we are more than conquerors through him who loved us. For I am convinced that neither death nor life, neither angels nor demons, neither the present nor the future, nor any powers, neither height nor depth, nor anything else in all creation, will be able to separate us from the love of God that is in Christ Jesus our Lord. (Rom. 8:37–39)

God loves you. Bad circumstances are not God withholding his love from you. You are not cursed. You are not unlucky. God has appointed you to be glorified into your calling. Your sins and mistakes are forgiven, so believe in that destiny. That change in your thinking will make all the difference in your outlook. Paul could testify personally to this, that though he faced so many challenges, God brought him through every time. God will bring you through too.

CAN SIN TAKE AWAY MY BLESSING?

When you are called by God to do his work, he gives you authority. This spiritual authority gives you power in your prayers, and it gives you the ability to fight spiritually against the darkness. As we submit to God's authority, we in turn keep the authority he has given us. But when we don't submit to what God wants us to do, we lose our authority.

Many people wrongly believe that when they sin, God is angry with them and has taken away their calling. They consider, *Perhaps with enough good behavior, he'll give it back.* I am glad to say without a doubt that your sin will not take away your destiny; however, it can cause major harm in your life. Aside from the fact that all our sin has earthly consequences to which we must make amends, it can also take away our spiritual authority.

It's not that God is punishing us or is angry with us. It's almost like chemistry: sin and heaven don't mix, and spiritual authority comes from heaven. So you can't live in sinful behavior and still operate with heavenly authority. It's like trying to microwave a burrito when the foil is still on. It won't work.

Imagine you had a million dollars in your checking account and were traveling out of state. You have your debit card, so you're not worried. You're able to use that card to make any purchase you want. But one day you lose your debit card and can't get your bank on the phone. At that point you haven't *lost* any money; you simply don't have access to it. When we sin or make mistakes, we don't lose our blessing; we simply temporarily lose our access to it. God will not wipe out your destiny because you've sinned. It's just that heavenly things and sin cannot coexist in the same space.

Get back on track and get your debit card back. Make amends with those you've hurt, and ask for forgiveness from God. It's that simple. He'll get you back on track. If you are still alive, God has not taken your blessing or destiny from you.

You may have done something really bad, something that hurt the people you love or is incredibly embarrassing. But it's during these times that you must look to God the most. The enemy wants you to wallow in shame for years; he wants you to fall into despair and to think God has turned his back on you. What you did was wrong, and it hurt people, but God is a friend of sinners. He can get you back on course to your destiny. God doesn't benefit from you punishing yourself and feeling shame all the time. He wants you to make things right with others.

DON'T DWELL ON SUFFERING

Suffering is part of life. When bad things happen to us, it's hard not to fall into despair and think, *God has left me*. It's during these times we might dwell on the past or on the mistakes we made, thinking, *If only I had done this differently.* We beat ourselves up or blame others. We fall into self-pity, thinking, *It will always be like this. I guess this is the new normal.*

It will not always be like this. God will get you through.

Don't dwell on your mistakes, and don't dwell on your imperfections. Don't dwell on all the bad things that might happen, because this trains your mind to worry. That will only make suffering worse.

Trying to control outcomes is a form of suffering because it never works the way we want. When we've been hurt enough times, we are tempted to control our colleagues, friends, and family members, to predict their motives and manipulate how they feel about us. We overplan for everything, living life in a perpetual state of worry. This kind of thinking is also suffering.

In fact, this can be the worst thing about going through trials. It's not the trial itself but the fear of another trial to come, dwelling on it, and trying to predict where it will come from next that beats us down. Maria Goff said, "It won't be the fires that destroy our lives and our faith. It will be obsessing over not getting burned again that will."[8]

Whatever you are going through now is temporary. It will get better. Don't try to predict where the next bad thing will come from, and don't constantly look for all the bad stuff so you can somehow keep it from happening.

Instead, look for what is good. Wait in expectation for good opportunities. God has already set things in motion; good things are coming your way. Don't be afraid. Build up your faith and your hope, and begin to see the best all around you. It's from the Lord, and it's for you.

Training

VERSE TO MEDITATE ON

"If we are faithless, he remains faithful, for he
cannot disown himself." (2 Tim. 2:13)

QUESTIONS TO CONSIDER

Grace and *favor* came from the same Greek word in the Bible; they are
interchangeable. How does that change my understanding of the words?
Do I believe God's grace/favor is a free gift by faith? Why or why not?

THOUGHT TO INHERIT

God favors me. Good things are coming.

DISCIPLINE TO PRACTICE

Practice gratitude. One of the best ways to open our spiritual eyes is to
see the many ways God is already blessing us. Sometimes when we get
in a rut, all we can see is the negative. But intentionally shifting our vision
to the good in our lives can help us see the greater good that is coming.

A recent study showed that the easiest way to increase a person's
happiness was to get them to write down five things they were thankful for once a day for twenty-one days. This simple practice dramatically
increased the feelings of happiness experienced by the test subjects, and
it lasted well after they stopped the practice.

This simple practice may be a good one for you. You can write it on a
cocktail napkin and throw it away. Or, if you're into social media, perhaps
you can post it online to keep yourself accountable by your peers. Who
knows, maybe they'll try it too. Either way, simply write down five things
you're thankful for. It doesn't matter how trivial.

CHAPTER 4

SELF-TALK AND SHAME

Define yourself radically as one
beloved by God. This is the true self.
Every other identity is illusion.

—BRENNAN MANNING

THOUGHT TO INHERIT: *I am the righteousness of God. I am his beloved.*

Brennan Hill was my best friend when we were growing up together in California. We did everything together. We were like brothers. Once we took a dinghy, a type of inflatable rowboat, into the local harbor and fished for hours, catching little halibut. We'd never seen anything like it. It was as if we'd won the jackpot, catching little one-to-two-pound fish schooling near the floating gas station near the rocks. We must have caught more than a hundred! We were over the moon. When we got back, I suppose we just assumed my dad would use them somehow.

"What's your plan with all those fish?" he asked.

We just looked at him blankly.

"If you kill a creature, you have to eat it. That's the rule." My dad made us clean more than a hundred halibut to get tiny little fillets for "popcorn fish." It took hours and was, in a way, horrible, but it will go down as one of my favorite memories.

Brennan and I had lots of memories like this. He was a tender-hearted kid who would often throw his arm around my shoulder, point at me, and say, "Bobby, you're my best friend." We spent nearly every summer together at the beach, fishing, or climbing the hills by his mom's house. He just loved everyone, especially his family.

While we were in junior high, Brennan's parents started having problems. I could tell it was getting to him, but we both just tried to ignore it. His dad wasn't around much, and his mom, who is the world's greatest person, was doing her best to stay positive and strong. Eventually, they got a divorce, and it destroyed Brennan. His behavior got progressively worse, but we remained great friends. By my second year of high school, when I moved to Oklahoma, we had lost contact. He went his way and I went mine.

Years later, as a married man, I moved back to California. The first person I called was Brennan. He looked very different—he had a shaved head and was super buff—but he seemed just as joyful as ever. We had a great time, but for whatever reason, I didn't hear much from him after that. That was almost twelve years ago.

Then, a few months ago, I got a direct message on Instagram from his sister:

> Hey Bobby, I don't know if u heard but Brennan died yesterday. Can you keep my family in your prayers? We are beyond broken. Took us by surprise to say the least.[1]

It's hard to explain the shock I felt. I hadn't seen Brennan in more than a decade, yet it felt like all the wind was taken out of my lungs when I read that. Apparently, he struggled with substance abuse but was working hard to beat it. One night, while watching TV, he paired pills with a couple of beers, and his heart stopped. He was thirty-five years old, with two kids.

When I got to the funeral, it almost felt like a family reunion. Everyone was so sad, but there was a sweetness in seeing all those old faces. I was invited to sit in the front with the family, but I just couldn't get a grip. I couldn't stop crying. I couldn't believe he was gone. I couldn't believe I hadn't called him or reached out to him. I'd never met his daughters. What kind of a friend was I?

At the reception his other sister sweetly said to me, "You know he always wanted to reconnect with you. He just wanted to get his life together first. He was embarrassed about the drugs."

This really got me. I think about this all the time because it's such a human emotion. We all feel it. "Let me get it all together, then I'll be worthy of a friend." I would have loved to have my old best friend back, drugs and all. Now he's gone.

BELONGING

The irony is that we need love and belonging the most when we are struggling. We need to know we are worthy of belonging, even with our imperfections. It's in connecting that we get the strength to overcome our challenges. The beautiful truth is that God loves us not as we should be but just as we are. We cannot do it alone. Over and over the Gospels show us how Jesus loved people exactly where they were—not some cleaned-up version of themselves, but who they were in their hurting, broken, neediest moments. We need him and we need our friends even when we don't have it all together.

SELF-TALK

So many of us say the worst things about ourselves. We bully our souls. Instead of affirming Scripture, we reinforce what the enemy says about us. That is to say, we disagree with God in our self-talk. When God says, "You are my beloved," the beloved child says, "No, I'm not enough."

- "I'm not attractive enough."
- "I'm an addict."
- "I'm a worthless sinner."
- "If people truly knew my secrets, they would reject me."
- "I'm a disappointment."
- "I'm disqualified."
- "I must hide things about myself."

When you speak this way to yourself, your enemy, the devil, is overjoyed, but your loving Father is grieved. He's not angry but rather proclaims something very different over you:

- "You are my beloved."
- "You are chosen."
- "You are forgiven, so forgive yourself."

SHAME

Shame is the habit of self-rejection that leads to a sinful life. You may have grown up believing that shame will, like psychological penance, cause you to become a better person. You think sin comes from pride, so therefore you must humiliate yourself to avoid sin. Hear this truth: such thinking is not helpful. It's harmful.

GUILT VERSUS SHAME

Shame is a deep sense of worthlessness and self-rejection. Shame means you're embarrassed about who you are. Guilt, on the other hand, is separate from the self. It's outside of who I am as a person. Guilt is the tension that happens when something I've done doesn't line up with who I know I am.

Guilt says, "I really messed up. I need to apologize and work toward a better solution. This is *not* who I am. I need to share my heart and ask for forgiveness." Shame says, "I'm a terrible person, and they will never love me again." Do you hear the difference?

So, guilt is separate from the self, and therefore, you can make amends, because it isn't *you*. In this way, when guilt is rightly understood and acted upon, it can be good for you. Shame is from the accuser, who says, "You're a total screwup and need to hide." And in this way, shame is never good.

> THE BEAUTIFUL TRUTH IS THAT GOD LOVES US NOT AS WE SHOULD BE BUT JUST AS WE ARE.

Guilt = I messed up. That's not me. Time to make it right.

Shame = I'm a screwup. I'm not worthy of belonging. Time to hide my flaws.

Though guilt can be great in helping you on your path to a holy life, shame will always lead you on a path to anxiety, depression, and sin. Shame always leads to sin. Always.

This role of shame leading to sin is especially apparent in the literature surrounding addiction theory. The graph below is the "Cycle of Addiction."

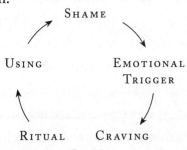

SHAME

USING   EMOTIONAL TRIGGER

RITUAL   CRAVING

Let's use the common example of an alcoholic; we'll call him Jim. Jim has seen the effects of alcohol abuse on his life. His wife is threatening to leave him. He's said some terrible things to his children that he didn't intend to say, and they are now uneasy around him. He's decided, *That's it! No more drinking*. He feels incredibly ashamed because of his behavior and can't live like this anymore.

Shame

The shame of Jim's behavior has him engaging in some pretty harsh inner monologue. He's saying things like, "I'm such a bad father. How could I have done this to my kids?" He's insecure and wonders if his wife will cheat on him or leave him because the fire just isn't in their relationship anymore. Of course it's not! He's not lovable after all he's done. This constant sense of shame is at the root of Jim's addiction. He's already lost the battle in his mind. Because of this kind of thinking and self-talk, he inevitably will go down the path that leads to more of the same behavior. Though he doesn't recognize it, his shame is functioning as a deep unconscious pain.

Emotional Trigger

One day Jim gets home late from work. He's been sober for two weeks and has been really working hard to save up some money. He wants to surprise his wife with a vacation to New York City, where they went on their honeymoon. He's sure this will mean the world to her, and maybe there they can draw closer to each other like when they were dating. As he comes through the door, Jim's wife starts yelling at him. She's been texting him, and he didn't respond. Dinner is cold, and "you always come home late even though I need you here." A fight ensues. This stressful experience functions as an emotional trigger for Jim because it reinforces his inner narrative of worthlessness.

Craving

The next day Jim has a huge craving for a drink. It's been there the whole time, but not like this. Work today just seems harder than it was, and he thinks, *Will my wife really even want to go to New York?* He's trying to get his emails done, but all he wants is just a small drink, you know, to take the edge off. This is hard, but he's determined to press through.

Ritual

On his way home, Jim takes a diversion. He decides to drive by his favorite bar, Joe's Tavern, where all his friends go after work. He's definitely not going to have a drink. He just wants to drive by and see how the old place is holding up. As he goes by, he sees one of his good friends outside having a cigarette. "Hey Jim! How the hell are you?" his friend says with a smile. Jim doesn't even stop, just rolls down the window. His friend quickly says, "Hey bud, hold on! I know you're done with drinking, but why don't you come in and say hi to the crew? You don't have to drink anything." He's feeling lonely and misses his friends, and of course there's no harm in just saying hi.

Using

The bartender puts his favorite beer in front of him. "Haven't seen you in a while, Jim. This one's on the house!" Overwhelmed with temptation but still strong, Jim says, "Oh thanks, but I'm sobering up." One of his other friends says, "Oh man, you're not going to get drunk from one beer. Just have one. It'll be fine!" He drinks one . . . then another, then four. Now he's on a bender. It feels so good to let go and be free.

Shame

Jim does something stupid. He drives home drunk. Stumbling into the house late at night, he finds his wife in the living room watching TV. She doesn't even say anything. She's been trying to call him, and now he comes home drunk. The next morning, he skips work and just lies in bed. He'll never beat this addiction. Why even try? He's a screwup like his dad.

• • •

Shame is at the heart of Jim's addiction. It's self-rejection. He believes the myth that he can control his addiction through willpower. This cycle of addiction is present everywhere. In my marginal and unprofessional opinion, most people are addicted to something. Though this type of graph is most often used for substance addictions, it applies to all our vices:

- Gambling
- Pornography/Sexual Addictions
- Workaholism
- Binge Shopping
- Eating Disorders/Overeating
- Cutting

Even exercise can be an addiction, though regrettably that is not one I struggle with.

The point remains: being ashamed about being fat won't help you control your eating. Being ashamed about your addiction to pornography won't break your behavior. All addictions (even those we don't always recognize, like compulsive TV watching) are rooted in shame. The pain of shame doesn't make you a better person. In fact, it ultimately makes your behavior worse, as it only leads to greater cravings and a deeper sense of ultimate loneliness.

How have most Christian churches helped in this regard? Some have been great, but most have not. Most have reinforced the nonbiblical legalistic idea that beating yourself up will somehow humble you and move you in the direction of holiness. It won't.

SHARING SHAME

Have you ever heard a pastor preach about "worthless, unlovable sinners"? I have! From the way some of them talk, everyone is going to hell. Not long ago I was having lunch with a friend who worked with one of these guys. I asked him, "Why is your boss so mean and legalistic?" He told me a story that touched my heart and even gave me compassion. The pastor had a rough childhood. His dad was incredibly strict and would hit and mock him as a child. When he was just a young boy, his father tied him up outside, hung a sign from his neck that read WORTHLESS, and left him there overnight as a punishment.

So many people who come across as heartless are actually struggling, perhaps unconsciously, with shame. The things they say to others—"You're worthless. You're a terrible sinner. You deserve to go to hell"—are things they say to themselves a thousand times over.

God loves even the unlovable. And God definitely loves you! God was overjoyed the day you were born. He was there to hear your first cry as a baby. He will be there to catch your last breath when you die. You are his beloved child, and he adores you. If you have little children, you likely love them very much. I love my kids so much, but not because of what they do. I don't say, "Haven, I love you because you made me this drawing." No, it's the other way around. I love the drawing because she is my heart. Nothing my kids could do could take away my love. If that's how I, a fallen and imperfect father, love my children, how much more does God love you?

THE TRUTH ABOUT SIN, JUDGMENT, AND HELL

I want to clarify that sin separates us from God, hell is a real place, and every person will face a very real judgment. But I also want to affirm the very good news that none of that is relevant for those who are in Christ Jesus. Because of Jesus we can approach the throne of God boldly, even though we've sinned.

We believe in Jesus' work on the cross and the resurrection, and that's all that matters. Then we build our lives in response to God's love with the help of the Holy Spirit. We make mistakes and will sin from time to time, and we feel guilty about that. But that's okay, because God's grace is big enough to save us and transform our hearts. "We do our best and forget the rest," as the saying goes.

God doesn't see you as a rotten sinner. You are his child, and he loves you. No one wants you to go to heaven more than God does. He can't wait to spend eternity with you. That's good news.

Keep in mind that the Greek word in the Bible that we translate as "grace" (*charis*) doesn't mean "mercy." It often feels that way. The way we describe grace makes it sound more like forgiveness when we mess up. But it's not. The most common definition of grace is "unmerited favor." Wait, favor—not mercy? Most lexicons have something even more inspiring. Grace is "that which affords joy, pleasure, delight, sweetness, charm, loveliness." Grace is "goodwill, loving-kindness, favor."[2]

This is so important. God's grace toward us is not just his mercy. It's not him giving us a free pass or letting us in even though he's angry. Rather, it's his abundant favor and his unending compassion toward us! We don't deserve it. We can't lose it. There's nothing we did to get it. Rather, it

> BECAUSE OF JESUS WE CAN APPROACH THE THRONE OF GOD BOLDLY, EVEN THOUGH WE'VE SINNED.

was bestowed on us through our faith in Jesus Christ, so it can never be taken from us. This grace then, as Dallas Willard put it, is like jet fuel for the disciples of Jesus.[3] His love gives us the power we need to live as Jesus did.

So, although shame always leads to sin, grace always leads organically and naturally to righteousness. Grace is patient. Grace is kind. Accept God's abundant grace. Forgive yourself. Be kind to your soul. You are so loved.

CONFESSION

It's good when new believers confess their sins when they come to faith in Jesus Christ. When those of us who have believed for a long time make mistakes, it's also good to confess those mistakes to the person we hurt or to someone who can pray with us and help us. But, though a popular practice in Bible churches like mine, we shouldn't constantly confess "I am a sinner" in the liturgical, thoughtless ways we often do. This is because after you're saved by grace through faith, you are no longer a sinner but the righteousness of God in Jesus.

Did you know that the apostle Paul, who wrote more of the New Testament books than any other single writer, never says to "confess your sins," or "confess you are a sinner"? Perhaps more than any other biblical writer, Paul laid out our understanding of what happens when a person is saved and remade in the kingdom of God. If confessing our sins is such an important part of our Christian journey, why did he never mention it? Why did Jesus never mention it?

Of course, it is in the Bible, but merely in two places. The book of James mentions it once (5:16) and the epistle of 1 John mentions it once (1:9). But again, why did Paul and Jesus never mention it if it's such an important practice?

Paul, of course, told the church to confess other things, like the lordship of Jesus Christ, the cross and resurrection, and that "there is now no condemnation for those who are in Christ Jesus, because through Christ Jesus the law of the Spirit who gives life has set you free from the law of sin and death" (Rom. 8:1–2). Confess that there is no condemnation for you. Paul taught people to confess their forgiveness, to confess their justification, and to confess their imputed righteousness, but he never told us to confess our sins. He wrote, "God made him who had no sin to be sin for us, so that in him we might become the righteousness of God" (2 Cor. 5:21). Wow!

Be honest about your sins, mistakes, and imperfections. Confess them to loving friends and ask for help. But also make sure to confess by faith your forgiveness, your favor, and, yes, your righteousness. It is a good and biblical thing to say, "I am the righteousness of God in Christ Jesus." When we confess these good and biblical things over our lives, our shame is replaced with God's love and joy. When this happens, the grip of sin and addiction in your life is loosened.

You may say, "I am not righteous at all. I'm a screwup and a sinner." What if, when we confess by faith, "I am a sinner," it becomes so? Or reverse that; what if when we confess by faith, "I am the righteousness of God," it becomes so?

Jesus was constantly proclaiming things "which be not as though they were" (Rom. 4:17 KJV), and they became so. He released his faith by speaking, and it changed the world around him. In one account, he went to heal a girl, but she had already died by the time he arrived. She was dead, but he said to the group, "She is not dead. She is sleeping." She was actually dead, and they began laughing at him. Then he took her by the hand and brought her back to life.

> Jesus called dead things alive, and they became so (Matt. 9:24–25).
> Jesus called lepers healed, and they became so (Mark 1:40–42).
> Jesus called you a new creation, and you became so (2 Cor. 5:17).
> Jesus calls sinners the righteousness of God, and they become so (2 Cor. 5:21).

Confess not that you're a dirty rotten sinner but that you are the righteousness of God. Do it every time you mess up, sin, or make a mistake. Watch how proclaiming the truth of the Bible will break the power of darkness in your life.

THE COURTHOUSE OF HEAVEN

Imagine you are in a courthouse of heaven and you are on trial. The Bible paints the picture that Jesus is your attorney, your "advocate," and the mangy devil is the prosecutor. He is, after all, called "the accuser of our brethren" (Rev. 12:10 KJV). The devil stands up, points directly at you, and says, "Your Honor, she is worse than she's ever been. She's hiding an addiction to pain pills; in fact, she stole the ones she has now. Have you seen her credit card bill? She can't stop shopping. And by the way, did you hear what she just said to her sister?"

Whose voice is life-giving? Whose voice brings death and destruction? Choose life! The Holy Spirit has been working to get you to confess the goodness of God in your self-talk. The enemy, the devil, wants you to condemn yourself, and he's using many churches to achieve that end. He knows that if you beat yourself up, you'll be stuck, but the Holy Spirit knows that if you believe you are loved and forgiven, you will receive the grace and time you need to heal.

Don't let people bully you. Don't bully yourself. You are loved. Zechariah says, "Whoever touches you touches the apple of the LORD's eye" (Zech. 2:8). It's as though God's love is so vast and deep for you that when someone pokes you or hurts you, they jab him in the eyeball. He just can't stand it.

I urge you to dwell on God's love and goodness. Reject thoughts of shame as the voice of the accuser. Forgive yourself. Don't be so hard on yourself. You're doing much better than you think, and you'll get where you're supposed to be.

Training

VERSE TO MEDITATE ON

"Therefore, there is now no condemnation for those who are in Christ Jesus, because through Christ Jesus the law of the Spirit who gives life has set you free from the law of sin and death." (Rom. 8:1–2)

QUESTIONS TO CONSIDER

What is the thing I will most likely beat myself up over? Has that self-talk helped or hurt? What is something God likes about me?

THOUGHT TO INHERIT

I am the righteousness of God. I am his beloved.

DISCIPLINE TO PRACTICE

Here I want to share a discipline with you that has totally changed my life. In fact, I wrote a whole book on putting this discipline into practice: *You Are Beloved*. I call it the Creed of the Beloved. I started saying the first part every time I prayed or went on retreat. I found myself saying this several times a day for a couple of months, and very quickly my thoughts changed, and, therefore, my behavior changed. No other discipline has had such a dramatic effect on my life.

Begin by saying the first half of the creed at least once a day before you pray. Perhaps say it a few times over and over so that it gets deep into your heart.[4] Say:

I'm not what I do,
I'm not what I have,
I'm not what people say about me,
I'm the beloved of God.

I believe if you put this into practice, within about two weeks you will see a measurable difference in how you feel and how you behave. This discipline frees us from legalism and sin management, and it helps us be better people through grace.

CHAPTER 5

FEELINGS VERSUS ACTION

Hard choices, easy life.
Easy choices, hard life.

—JERZY GREGOREK

THOUGHT TO INHERIT: *I can break through*
overthinking by taking action now.

I t's hard to take action in life when we just don't feel like it. Overthinking is usually the culprit. We think about how much work it will be, we imagine all the bad things that could happen if we launch a new project, and we think about all the other stuff that sounds a lot more fun or relaxing. It's been said that emotions make great slaves but terrible masters. When we are feeling joyful, in love, excited, or like everything in life is going really well, emotions are great. Those positive feelings help us get up in the morning and feel like doing our work, spending time with our kids or grandkids, or going the extra mile for others. But what happens when our emotions take a turn for the worse, when we feel lazy, or even depressed, and we can't seem to make the progress we need or want? What happens when we get lethargic, apathetic, or just don't feel like doing the thing we need to do?

In these times, overthinking allows those negative emotions to become our master. We think and think and ultimately find a way to avoid the thing we need to do. We procrastinate and file the thing away to be done at another time. We need to go to the gym, apply for a new job, or try a new church, but today we just don't feel like it. At times like these, thinking too much can get in the way. We spin our wheels and do the opposite of what we've set out to do.

Overthinking can become a real problem in life, because when opportunity strikes, we are more likely to miss out. When God opens an amazing door, we may blow it because we didn't feel like going to that interview or making that phone call. We may miss that one connection that could change everything. Of course, the world is full of limitless opportunities, but to benefit from that opportunity, we need to not only see an opportunity but also act on it. We need to be the kind of person who has a bias toward action before overthinking allows us to kill the opportunity itself.

There are these key moments in life when opportunity comes and we are like the five virgins with oil in our lamps, ready to join the party (Matt. 25: 1–13). Much of the success in our lives is because we jumped onto something great, something we knew we couldn't miss out on. Look back at your life, and you'll see that some of your greatest achievements boiled down to taking a risk. Perhaps there are places in your life where you can say, "Yeah, things would be better if I had acted, if I had only done the thing I knew I should have done."

This has happened in my life a lot. I have missed out on major opportunities because, though I knew they were good, I procrastinated and missed out on the party. But other times, when I had a bias toward action and made a decision before I could think myself out of it, I could clearly see amazing results. Had I not moved at those times, my life would not be as good as it is today.

THE THINGS WE DO FOR LOVE

The best example of this is when I started dating the love of my life, Hannah. As I mentioned earlier, at age sixteen I moved to Tulsa, Oklahoma, and it was there at church I saw a girl. A friend of mine introduced me to her, and the second I saw Hannah I was in love. Not only was (and is) she beautiful, but I knew then that she was the one I was destined to be with. Love at first sight is not for everyone, but I know it was right for me. God wanted me to be with her. At the time, I wasn't thinking so spiritually. I just really liked her and wanted to date her.

However, she was with another guy. Years went by, and I still had this big crush on Hannah. I was friends with her brother, so our paths would cross from time to time, but whenever I talked to her I got sheepish and couldn't speak coherently. All this time she was dating this same guy; I dated other girls, but honestly, she was the only one I ever wanted to be with. This went on for years until finally, in college, the window opened.

It was the beginning of summer, and I was invited by her brother to go on a missionary trip to Panama. Hannah came too, and I got to know her a little better and found out she was single again! At the end of the trip, I told her and another friend, Natasha, they should come out to my dad's place in California to get out of the Oklahoma heat. That little seed eventually led to Hannah, her brother, Chris, and another mutual friend of ours, Nate, all coming to visit me.

Of course, I laid it on thick. I talked to her as much as I could. I tried to arrange our schedule so that Chris and Nate would be busy so I could get alone time with Hannah. And sure enough, the chemistry started happening. I could tell, just maybe, that Hannah was interested in me.

By the end of their visit, I thought things were going pretty well. Chris was to be married in a few days, and they were all getting excited for the wedding. I wasn't planning on attending since I typically spent the whole summer in California and the wedding was in Tulsa. Then Hannah threw out this little comment: "It's too bad you're not going to my brother's wedding. It would be fun to see you again."

In a matter of about two seconds, I realized Hannah was interested in me, but she was going back to Tulsa where I wouldn't see her for almost two months. There were lots of good-looking guys who were interested in her back in Oklahoma, including her old boyfriend (who I'm sure wasn't over her). I needed to see her again soon or this opportunity would slip away.

"I'll tell you what," I said. "If you agree to give me either the first dance or the last dance at the reception, I will come out to your brother's wedding." Keep in mind, I was nineteen and I had no money at all. I had no idea how I was going to get to Tulsa. Buying a plane ticket days before you need to go somewhere is incredibly expensive, and I was sure I didn't have the money. All I knew was this was my chance, the one I'd been waiting for, for years. It was now or never, and I was going to find a way to get out there and get that dance, even if I had to start walking.

Hannah's response? "I'll tell you what," she said. "If you come out to my brother's wedding, I'll give you both."

I did get out to the wedding, and I got the first dance, the last dance, and all the dances in between. After that wedding, Hannah and I started dating. Talking about it recently, we agreed that if I hadn't gone out to Tulsa and struck while the iron was hot, we probably wouldn't have dated and eventually married. I'm sure in those two months or so that were left of summer, another guy would have come along. I'm so glad I acted, I went, and I didn't overthink. I didn't figure out first if I could get there, and I didn't plan it all out. I just knew this was my chance, and I acted.

Of course, impulsive decisions can have negative ramifications—especially if they're made out of wrongly held beliefs about who we are. But most often in unhappy people I've seen a "paralysis of analysis." That's what makes us miss out on key opportunities. Sometimes taking hold of a moment has to happen quickly and we don't always have time to think through everything. Fear, anxiety, and procrastination set in, and we kill the idea or opportunity.

JUMP!

A few years ago my brother led my friends and me on this thing we called "the coastal challenge" in California. It was a ten-mile run, climb, and swim, starting on the southern coast in San Clemente and working its way north all the way to Main Beach in Laguna Beach. This really was a challenge, as working around the waves and rocks would leave many of us bleeding and bruised.

The climax of the event was when my brother took us to a shortcut. In order to avoid swimming around "the point," he walked us up a steep hill that led to a cliff about forty-five feet above the ocean. Standing up there, I said to him, "Oh, bummer. A dead end."

"Dead end?" he said. "No man, we're jumping off of this." It was so high I felt like a fair maiden from an English novel who was about to romantically jump off the cliff to her death.

"Anthony, you can't jump off this; it's way too high."

"Bobby, you totally can. I've done it before," he said.

"No way, you'll—" And then he did it. In the middle of my sentence he jumped off the cliff, and in mid-air, falling, he turned around and stuck his tongue out at me. I was sure he was going to die.

Looking down, I saw him, safe and sound. Up top, we were

looking at one another dumbly. Now, this is the point I want you to get. All of us were adult men. Having been through similar situations throughout our lives, we knew one thing and one thing alone: if we were going to jump off this cliff, it was now or never. When I say *now*, I mean *right now*. Anyone who would stand up there looking down for more than, say, five to ten seconds would lose the momentum and courage to jump. I'm happy to say, because we corporately understood this universal truth, all of us jumped as quickly as possible. Yes, it was super high, and yes, it hurt when I landed. Do I regret it? No! I have a memory of a thrilling moment and a reinforced belief about my own abilities.

FIVE SECONDS

When opportunity comes in life and you need to act, overthinking can kill a good idea. In fact, it usually does. This is the main point of the great work by Mel Robbins called *The 5 Second Rule*. Robbins gives some very convincing evidence that if you wait more than five seconds to do something you're supposed to do, your brain will kill the idea. If you don't marry your idea to a specific action within those five seconds, it will likely go nowhere. To combat that, she recommends the practice of counting down quickly out loud—"5 . . . 4 . . . 3 . . . 2 . . . 1 . . ."—and doing the thing you're supposed to do. This simple practice will train you to have a bias toward acting.[1]

She stumbled upon this great practice by accident. She's not sure how it happened, but somehow she got to a place in life where everything was going wrong. She left a lucrative legal practice to pursue being a TV show host. The show got canceled and she was still tied up in a contract, so she was unable to pursue any other media career until the one-year clause was over. Media was her dream, and she didn't want to go back into law.

Pair this with the fact that her husband had started a restaurant that was struggling at the same time. It was bleeding, and they were running out of money. She'd had a negative balance in her checking account for months, and they were way behind on their mortgage. The bank was starting to call, and she was feeling totally overwhelmed. Her marriage was starting to fall apart under the pressure of it all. It was during this time that she started hitting the snooze button.

Every morning when the alarm went off, she knew what she needed to do. She needed to get up, work out, get dressed, get the kids to school, and go out and find a job. But every day, for months, she would hit the snooze button over and over. By the time she would actually get up, she was way behind. The kids missed the bus, she skipped her workout, she ate breakfast in the car, and all day she was in constant catch-up mode.

One night she saw a commercial with a rocket ship taking off that had that long countdown: "5 . . . 4 . . . 3 . . . 2 . . . 1 . . . lift off!" She said to herself, *Tomorrow morning I'm going to count down from five and get out of bed.* Believe it or not, it worked! She started applying this practice every time she needed to do something but didn't feel like it. She'd quietly count to herself,

"5 . . . 4 . . . 3 . . . 2 . . . 1 . . . get dressed for yoga."
"5 . . . 4 . . . 3 . . . 2 . . . 1 . . . call that guy and apply for the job."
"5 . . . 4 . . . 3 . . . 2 . . . 1 . . . get the kids dressed for school."

Robbins's book contains scientific studies showing that, unless you marry it with a *specific action*, in five seconds an idea will die. She shows how counting down from five shifts the way your mind thinks, and it connects the goal with the action of counting down.

It sounded silly to me at first, but it works. There are many times in my life when I don't feel like turning off the TV and running that errand, or calling someone back I know I need to call. I'll say to myself, "5 . . . 4 . . . 3 . . . 2 . . . 1 . . . call John." It works; try it sometime.

It's so good to train ourselves into a bias toward action and to become a doing person. Rather than thinking yourself out of action, the next time a great opportunity comes in your life, don't overthink. Act.

BE A DOER

If it's going to be, it's up to you. No one is going to make it happen for you. You have to choose daily to move in the direction of the vision for your life. No matter how you feel emotionally, you really do have the ability to make the right choices for your life.

NO MATTER HOW YOU FEEL EMOTIONALLY, YOU REALLY DO HAVE THE ABILITY TO MAKE THE RIGHT CHOICES FOR YOUR LIFE.

There's something great about knowing *I can do what I choose to do, even though the emotions in my head are pushing me in another direction.* I can choose to smile even if my body hurts. I can choose to get up in the morning even if I feel depressed. I can choose to be vulnerable and authentic and get help for my addiction. I can even choose to be nice when I'm hungry.

For instance, the other day I was driving and got frustrated. "Hannah, do we turn left here or what?" I asked somewhat harshly.

"Yes," she answered. Then, "Bobby, have you eaten yet?" she asked kindly. My wife's loving response prompted me to get my emotions in check. I had a choice about how to behave, despite how I might feel emotionally.

FEELINGS CAN RUN YOUR LIFE—IF YOU LET THEM

Moving toward what we really want for our lives (even though we don't emotionally feel like it) is tough. But every time we do it, we recognize we have more power over our emotions than we thought. That's both freeing and empowering. Therefore, never allow your emotions to dictate your destiny. Train your emotions to come in line with your vision for your life.

When I need to be assertive, I choose to drum up courage in my heart. When I'm feeling lazy and don't want to be social, I tap into emotions of joy and mirth to be more engaging with the people I love. It's not always possible, but often you can decide to feel the emotions that will be a blessing to others, emotions like joy, cheerfulness, and empathy. They can be trained into your thinking. You can choose to feel them by applying your will.

No matter what your parents, professors, or friends have told you, you are not the result of your environment. You are the result of your choices, and your choices are the result of your thinking. If you overthink and spin your wheels, you'll stay stuck. You can do whatever you apply yourself to, despite the emotions you feel when you're getting started. If it's going to happen, you'll need to make it happen. You can do this!

A LESSON FROM GRANDPA SCHULLER

My Grandpa Schuller was an amazing man. He founded the *Hour of Power*, the ministry I currently lead. Many in my generation have no idea who he was, but he was truly a powerhouse for the kingdom of God. He was passionate about developing "possibility thinkers," men and women of God who would dream big. He wanted people to see that the world was an environment of endless possibilities, and that if you could only see them, you could accomplish great things for God too.

My grandpa was such a wonderful grandpa to all of the grandkids. He gave huge bear hugs. He was so available, compassionate, and really encouraging. But I'm embarrassed to admit that, when I was in high school, I thought my grandpa was at best "off-track" and at worst a heretic.

I never told him my thoughts about his off-track theology, and I'm thankful. He didn't deserve the criticism I would have given, though he may have been amused to hear it. At the time I had just come to faith. I was about seventeen and had plugged in with some Holiness churches in Tulsa. They were great communities, but they could be very rigid. Perhaps as a teenager this is where God wanted me, in a community with strict rules and guidelines about how to be a moral teenager. Still, my peers and pastors had a low opinion of Dr. Schuller and his "New Age" positive-thinking mumbo jumbo. At the time I agreed with them. "He doesn't preach sin. He doesn't give altar calls," and so on.

But the summer after my junior year, I went on a fishing trip with him. He could see my heart for Jesus and really wanted to nurture it. I could tell he wanted me to be a pastor. He would flatly say it. Though my dad, also a pastor, encouraged us kids to pursue whatever we wanted vocationally and gave us zero pressure to go into ministry, my grandpa adamantly wanted me to follow in my dad's footsteps.

On this fishing trip, he was trying to train me to preach. He handed me a copy of his latest book, titled *If It's Going to Be, It's Up to Me!* On the boat we were trolling jigs behind us (those colorful plastic toys that look like squid), which meant we'd be sitting around for hours, trudging along, hoping to catch a big tuna or a marlin. Those could be boring afternoons, so it was there he thought to make practical use of our time.

"Read the title of the book to me," he said.

"If it's going to be, it's up to me," I said in an I'm-too-cool-for-this teenager voice.

"No!" he said, this time getting frustrated, standing up quickly, wobbly legged inside the cabin as the boat rocked back and forth. "Read it with passion!"

"If it's going to be, it's up to me!" This time I said it with my own version of passion. I thought I'd be a sport and see where this was going.

"No! With *real* passion! Please!"

This time I did it more like I was rehearsing for *Macbeth*, mustering up as much energy as I could. It was still not good enough. I was getting annoyed.

The fourth time I was going to get him off my back. I would do my own Dr. Schuller caricature. I did it slowly, boldly, arms flailing, eyes glazed as if I was nearly about to weep. I said it in a deep, deep Dr. Schuller voice and finished with the corniest smile I could muster.

"Perfect! Perfect!" At this point I'm pretty sure he didn't get that I was teasing him. This perturbed me more than I care to describe.

"Take the book, Bobby. Read it. You can have it."

To be honest with you, the title of this book bothered me to no end. As I already mentioned, I had my concerns about my grandpa being a heretic, and this book title wasn't helping things. "If it's going to be, it's up to me?" Shouldn't it say, "If it's going to be, it's up to God"?

This title bothered me so much that when I got home I started reading it. I was reading it, not to learn, but to critique. How proud and foolish I was! I was like one of those legalistic pastors who decide to read another pastor's book they're jealous of so they can tell their congregants all the things wrong in it. But thanks be to God, something else happened.

I got it. I understood what he was doing. He was teaching the power and the importance of personal choice. He wanted people to know they could get unstuck if they only chose to move against their emotions, to not be victims, and to not wallow in self-pity. He wanted people to see that God is on their side and wants to do great things through them. I began to see that my grandpa didn't write for theologians or even Christians. He wrote for hurting people who needed a personal touch from God. He wrote so people could have hope. He wanted people to see that they could will themselves to a new destiny despite how they were feeling. He needed people to know they had a choice.

DONE DEAL

To this day, I love the phrase, "If it's going to be, it's up to me." It's better than, "If it's going to be, it's up to God." Here's why: God has already done it. We need to choose to respond. God has already called your destiny blessed. Reach out and grab it. God is not currently deciding. He's already decided. Now, how will you respond? Will you reach out to your destiny, or will you wallow in self-pity? Will you take the next step, or will you procrastinate? God's already done the hard part. Now, truly, if it's going to be, it's up to you.

It's like this. Imagine Bill Gates called and said, "I want to make a donation of a million dollars to the cause of your choice. All I ask in return is that you take me out to lunch. Take me anywhere you like, and I'll hand you a check for a million dollars."

At that point, is the million-dollar gift up to Bill Gates? No! In a very real way, it's up to you!

Bill Gates has the money; he's wired for giving to good causes; he'll do what he said he would do. The choice is now yours: Will you call and make that lunch appointment? If it's going to be, it will be up to you.

YOU HAVE A CHOICE

Thinking, *If it's going to be, it's up to this person, that person, this group, that boss, or that organization*, will never lead you to a successful life. Thinking, *If it's going to be, it's up to me*, makes all the difference. No matter how bad things get, no matter how sick, broke, messed up, or addicted you are, you always have a choice. Giving up your ability to choose is soul-killing because it's giving up the very thing that makes you human. Choice is the thing that separates us from the animals. Animals have to do simply what their instinct tells them. Their destinies are completely tied to their nature. When we believe we are stuck and don't have a choice, we feel as though we are slaves, animals, at the mercy of fate.

The truth is that our lives are filled with limitless possibility, and with possibility comes choices. Like the man who sits in prison, falsely accused: though he doesn't want to be there, he decides to read, to grow, to exercise, and to find out what went wrong with his case. He has a choice.

NO MATTER HOW BAD THINGS GET, NO MATTER HOW SICK, BROKE, MESSED UP, OR ADDICTED YOU ARE, YOU ALWAYS HAVE A CHOICE.

Or like the kid who grows up in a rough part of town: All of his friends are getting into gangs and street life. They tell him it's his only choice, that he has to do this to survive. But instead he applies himself to school, he gets involved with his church, and he chooses to get into a great college, despite his environment. He knows he has many choices and, therefore, many possibilities.

Even the most helpless of people are not truly helpless. The drug addict who realizes she can't get clean on her own and finally reaches out for help. That, too, is a choice, and it makes all the difference. Or the woman who wants to take her life and calls a friend instead. She looks back at that moment later in her life and is so glad she did.

You don't have to stay stuck where you are. Thoughts of helplessness are contagious. If you get around enough people who all say the same thing—"You have to stay stuck here"—you start to believe it. God has a great destiny for your life, but you have to let go of being helpless to access it. Choose today to move forward.

Sometimes we become like the circus elephants of the past who were unaware of their own strength. It's said that when baby circus elephants were being domesticated, owners tied the baby elephant's leg to a stake in the ground. When the baby elephant tried to run after something interesting, or perhaps escape, its foot would be caught by the tie. After enough time, the spirit of the animal was broken.

In time, the baby elephant grew to enormous size and tremendous strength. Full-grown elephants can pull entire trees out of the ground by the roots. They can stomp and throw predators with ease. But this humungous, powerful elephant, so accustomed to being tethered by a small stake, wouldn't even try to escape. These broken elephants didn't need to be put in cages. Just the sight of the little stake in the ground defeated them mentally. They were merely prisoners of their thoughts.

What's your stake in the ground? Like that elephant, you have more strength than you know. Perhaps your spirit feels broken, and when you see your stake you become immobilized, thinking, *I have no choice. I have to stay here.* Perhaps it's a job you hate. Maybe you have a boss who is harassing you, and you think you have no choice but to put up with it. Maybe you're in a relationship that's abusive, but you feel like no one will want you if you leave. Maybe there's a project on your heart you've never pursued because it means other, more lucrative things will have to be put on the back burner. Just remember, though you feel emotional about these things, don't lose the mental game. You have a choice.

THE COST OF POWER

It costs us something when we choose. In their book *Willpower,* Roy Baumeister and John Tierney point out that we lose mental energy every time we make a choice.[2] When we choose whether or not we will go out with our friends or work on that lingering project, it takes energy. When we have to choose who we will vote for, where we will go to church, or whether our kids will get into that new program, we expend energy. Even when we order food at a restaurant, it costs us energy. Sometimes we choose not to choose to preserve energy. But that, too, has a cost.

In addition to the willpower and energy it takes to choose, we intuitively recognize that each choice has consequences. It's been said, "Every choice is a thousand renunciations."[3] That's the scary part. When I chose to become a husband, I renounced every other woman on earth for the rest of my life. When I chose to become a father, I renounced having a good night's sleep for eighteen years. Becoming a family man, I renounced my bachelor life (and I'm glad for it). Still, it's a loss of some freedoms and time that could be spent traveling the world or working more on my hobbies, for example. To start your own business, you lose the safety of a stable job. To leave a toxic boyfriend, you lose the chance of having a family with him this year. Even becoming a Christian means renouncing certain worldly behaviors and practices to inherit a new life. With every decision we make, we receive something, but we lose something as well. This is why so many people are indecisive. They prefer not to make a choice because the pain of leaving one thing to inherit the other is too great.

CHOOSE TODAY!

Perhaps as you're reading this something is stirring inside of you. You know there's a choice you need to make but it will be the beginning of a long, arduous journey. Perhaps it feels scary or exhausting, so the temptation is to continue to wait, to procrastinate as you always have. Perhaps you need to make a choice today. Perhaps you need to do something even now to "burn the ships," to force yourself to make the difficult decision you know you should have made a long time ago.

It's very common for God to lay these life-altering choices before us. When he does, he says, "Choose today!" When the people of Israel were brought out of Egypt, they went through many difficult challenges. Finally, they inherited the promised land God swore to give them. Before they entered, Joshua gathered all the elders and leaders of Israel at a place called Shechem and said:

> "So I gave you a land on which you did not toil and cities you did not build; and you live in them and eat from vineyards and olive groves that you did not plant."
>
> Now fear the LORD and serve him with all faithfulness. Throw away the gods your ancestors worshiped beyond the Euphrates River and in Egypt, and serve the LORD. But if serving the LORD seems undesirable to you, then choose for yourselves this day whom you will serve, whether the gods your ancestors served beyond the Euphrates, or the gods of the Amorites, in whose land you are living. But as for me and my household, we will serve the LORD. (Josh. 24:13–15)

Many of the Jewish people were trying to have it both ways. They wanted to serve the gods of their ancestors or some pagan gods they thought had perhaps brought them luck, but they also wanted to serve Yahweh. Finally, Joshua, their leader, set a choice before them. It was one or the other, and they had to choose "this day"!

I want to encourage you. If there's a big choice you need to make, make it now. If it's God's idea, it will be so worth it. He always has our best in mind and always pushes us to be better than we were yesterday. The uncomfortable tension you feel between where you are now and where you want to be is a good thing. Take some time to recognize that you can choose today to be in a different place. Don't allow emotions to rob you of your destiny.

Training

VERSE TO MEDITATE ON

"Where there are no oxen, the manger is empty,
but from the strength of an ox come abundant harvests."
(Prov. 14:4) What does this verse mean to you?

QUESTION TO CONSIDER

What is an action I can take in the next twenty-four hours
that will move me in a better direction for my life?

THOUGHT TO INHERIT

I can break through overthinking by taking action now.

DISCIPLINE TO PRACTICE

Try Mel Robbins's five-second rule for yourself. When I did it, I was shocked at how well it worked. Believe it or not, she has some very convincing research to show that the practice really will make a big difference. Try it sometime this week and watch how compelling it is. You'll not only enjoy having this new tool in your toolbox, but you'll also see the negative impact overthinking has had on your life.

CHAPTER 6

BUILDING A VISION FOR YOUR LIFE

*If you don't have a vision for
the future, then your future is
threatened to be a repeat of the past.*
—A. R. BERNARD

W hat would you dare to achieve if you knew you could not fail?" I remember hearing my granddad ask this question. He was the ultimate dreamer. And I watched how, unlike most dreamers, he was able to consistently achieve what most people thought impossible. As a young rural pastor, he was able to get Norman Vincent Peale to come out to his church all the way from New York even though everyone said, "He'll never come to your little drive-in movie-theater church." When the Soviet Union was arresting missionaries who were taking Bibles into their country, he was able to convince the Soviet government to broadcast his sermons every week to the whole country. And of course, he wanted to build a gigantic glass cathedral with ten thousand windows, and he did. The difference between my grandpa and most other dreamers is that he was an idealist.

He didn't just dream. He wanted everything to be the best and most excellent it could be. He had a crystal-clear picture for how his services should be, how his ministry culture should be, and what it meant to win or lose as an organization. He was almost neurotic about how the Crystal Cathedral campus should look. The windows always had to be clean. People weren't allowed to use paper signs anywhere for any reason. He wanted it to be aesthetically pleasing down to the smallest detail.

My granddad's idealism wasn't mean-spirited. On the contrary, it was uncannily positive. It was inspiring. And people knew that it was about something greater than Dr. Schuller or his ministry. It was about reaching unchurched people with excellence. I'll always admire him because he refused to settle for anything less than what he pictured, but he was able to do it in a positive way, encouraging people and helping his team achieve what most called impossible. We can all be this way.

He used to say, "Build your dream, and your dream will build you." This axiom is so true. In a book about changing our thoughts, this is perhaps one of the most vital shifts in our thinking. Build a dream for your family, your vocation, and your walk with God. Though your dream may change over time, simply having a clear picture of what you want to be and what you want to achieve will dramatically alter your character and sense of well-being for the better.

I am not ashamed to say I am an idealist. This doesn't mean I'm rigid or that I'm legalistic. It simply means I have a clear picture of what is ideal for my life, my family, and my church, and I work diligently to get there. I'm at peace with the fact that I'm not where I want to be, yet I am constantly painting the ideal for our ministry to our team so we never become complacent with where we are.

As a positive idealist, I ask others to help shape my vision. I encourage others to form clear visions for their own lives as well. In this way, the idealism we share as a team or as a family is positively reinforced and, therefore, more likely to succeed. Idealism and dreaming are two sides of the same coin. Dreaming reinforces our ideals, and forming principles (ideals) helps us achieve our dreams.

CHERISH YOUR DREAMS

Every one of us starts out a dreamer. We're born to be visionary, but sometimes we lose our way. That's why, when we aren't a part of a vision, it's easy to feel kind of dead. Spiritually dead visionaries feel shame about the fact that they aren't where they truly want to be. To cope with their shame, they try to pull down others who give voice to their own dreams. Don't let them get to you. They are hurting. They have been wounded by life. And most of all, they are wrong. If you have a dream, if you write it down, if you stay persistent and allow others to give you feedback, you can accomplish almost anything. You are limited only by your thoughts.

We're born with an innate desire to create. Children dream of their futures from the time they can talk! But in time, most people have let their dreams die. For some, they've allowed ridicule from parents or friends to rob them of their destiny. For others, they failed too many times and just couldn't find the strength to conjure another dream. Still others found that the pursuit of those dreams was a volatile thing, and they gave in to pressure from society to pick a safer option. Though everyone has their reasons for why they dropped out of school, gave up on getting married, or left a business venture, losing a dream is extremely painful.

> IF YOU HAVE A DREAM, IF YOU WRITE IT DOWN, IF YOU STAY PERSISTENT AND ALLOW OTHERS TO GIVE YOU FEEDBACK, YOU CAN ACCOMPLISH ALMOST ANYTHING.

What's more painful, however, is living life without any vision or dream whatsoever. If you don't have a dream in your heart, falling into depression or monotony becomes easy. Dreams are like oxygen! When you have a big dream, something inside of you begins to stir. You feel young again. You feel like life can and will change for you. In this way, dreams are soul nourishing and refreshing. Even if we don't accomplish those dreams, merely having them will drive us to do more, be better, and grow.

BEFRIEND BIG DREAMERS

Have you ever been in a room full of dreamers? It's so inspiring. It's amazing to hear people talk about what the future could look like through the companies or nonprofits they are building. I love gathering with pastors as well, because most pastors are dreamers, always thinking of ways they can communicate the good news in a fresh way to people who have never heard it.

It's important that you don't spend too much time with people who want to tear down your dreams and goals. Though it's good to allow peers to critique you so that your ego does not keep you from improving, stay away from people who love to use the word *impossible*. That word is irresponsible and lazy. It does very little to help others, and it nearly always comes from a place of fear, ignorance, and pride.

Instead, seek out the company of dreamers as if your life depended on it. What if five years from now your life is completely different because you were intentional about the friends you made and the books you read? The friends we have and the books we read shape our thoughts, and our thoughts become our future. The company we keep shapes our view of the world. When you are around dreamers and positive idealists who are achieving great things, you will begin to achieve more too. Just from talking with them and being with them, you will find yourself broadening your vision for who you could be and what you could accomplish.

We know this intuitively. Parents of a child who has gone down a wrong path will often say, "He's a good kid, but he just got tied up with the wrong group of friends." That's because we know friends influence each other, sometimes to their detriment.

This is true for adults as well as teenagers! Why are we so reluctant to follow the good advice we give our children? If I want my kids to be around good kids, shouldn't I be closest to people I want to be like too? Shouldn't I spend a good amount of time with people I respect and admire? Though we should always care for and love our neighbors who are in need, our deepest and closest friendships should be with the people we want to emulate. When we spend time with dreamers and positive idealists, we are choosing to take on their kind of thinking, and in the end, that changes everything.

INVITE OTHER DREAMERS TO COME ALONG

When you have a group of friends who are positive idealists or dreamers, share your dream with them. Sharing your dream can be scary because you are asking others to critique your dream and determine whether you can achieve it. They may say it's a stupid idea, suggest a shift, or even laugh. That kind of response can be painful, but in the end it is always good because it can help you see blind spots you'd rather ignore. This process helps you discern whether your dream is a good one.

But the opposite can happen as well, and when it does it is magic. You tell your dream or vision to someone, and it starts to take greater shape. Your friend may get wide-eyed and say something like:

"That's amazing."
"What if that could really happen?"
"Can I come along?"

And when that happens you have not only a dream; you have a believer who might come alongside you. Your dream has now become a vision that others may follow.

Saying your dream out loud is so important because no dream comes to pass without being pitched. In fact, every great dream ever has had to be pitched over and over to multiple people. When pitching an idea, you constantly get information, not all of it good, and feedback that will help you improve your pitch each time around.

SAYING YOUR DREAM OUT LOUD IS SO IMPORTANT BECAUSE NO DREAM COMES TO PASS WITHOUT BEING PITCHED.

Every time you talk about it with someone, you will see which bits get people excited and which parts are boring. This is a necessary part of the refining process for your idea.

Another reason why pitching your idea to a friend is a vital first step is because it keeps you accountable to actually do something. If you say, "I want to go back to college and get a degree in engineering," the next time you see them, they'll ask if you've applied yet. The brutal reality of saying no is both painful and good for you. If they're a dreamer and a good friend, they'll keep pestering you to apply. Those are the best kinds of friends, even though they can be annoying. Just remember that a friend who pushes you to be better and to achieve your goals is a friend who believes in you and loves you.

If it's been a while since you've had a big, crazy, awesome goal or dream, and you want one, here are some suggestions of things you can dream about:

A Vision for Your Loved Ones

Recently we went on a family vacation; it was the first in a long time. We were at the end of the third year of fighting for my son Cohen's health. He has a brain malformation that causes epilepsy and some behavioral issues. The struggle has been difficult for all of us, most of all Cohen. Though he was five at the time, he had the mind of a two-year-old. He was still in diapers and didn't play well with other children. Much of his days were spent in therapy of some kind or another. But more than that, we had several trips to the hospital, some of which were paired with long nights of wondering if this seizure or that seizure was going to take his life or disable him further. There are no words to describe how painful, taxing, and scary this has been for our family. To say the least, we were exhausted, so we took a vacation.

Because Cohen was heavily dependent on his rhythms and structure at home to be comfortable, he stayed home with his grandma while we traveled to Hawaii. Though this tough decision to go without him made the trip more relaxing, it also gave it a touch of sadness. Would we ever be able to go on vacation with our son?

As we were walking around the hotel and along the beach, Hannah began asking our seven-year-old daughter, Haven, about Cohen, drawing out her feelings. As Haven began to talk, she started crying. "I feel like I don't really have a brother," she said. "I want to play with him, but he doesn't know how to play. He just breaks things. I want a brother I can be friends with, but Cohen doesn't understand anything." She cried some more. We realized

Haven had been bottling up these feelings. There we were, three of the four of us, on vacation without our little buddy.

The next day, after having a quiet time and reading some of Stephen Covey's books, Hannah came up with a great idea. She said, "We should have a vision for our family." After all, if vision creates life, a vision for our family would bring life to our family experience. So Hannah and I, during a tropical rainstorm at the hotel, sat on the covered porch in rocking chairs and put together a dream for our family. When we finished, we talked with Haven and asked her to help us make it better, and she did. Here's the vision we came up with for the Schuller family:

1. We won't allow setbacks to keep us from enjoying each other.
2. We will be a family that worships Jesus.
3. Christian character is our highest value.
4. We show strength by being vulnerable with each other.
5. Leadership means serving others.
6. Family is first. Family is forever.
7. We will support and develop one another's talents.
8. We will never stop believing in miracles.

The last one was Haven's, and it's my favorite. It's a way of saying we will always be a family that dreams and believes.

I can say without a doubt that making this list was a great idea. Having a vision for what we want our family to be, and applying that vision, made us all feel closer to one another. It has helped the three of us endure the challenges with our beloved son (he's doing much better, by the way, though at the time of this writing he still has a ways to go).

Casting a vision for anything breathes life into that thing.

Whether you're married or single, newly married, divorced, whatever, it's important to imagine your ideal future with your loved ones. Once you do, you'll begin living into the future you envision. Casting a vision for how your relationships will be tomorrow and ten years from now is powerful! Take the initiative. Share it with those you love when the time is right, and even ask them to speak into it. The important thing is that *you* begin to dream today.

A Vision for Personal Growth

Having a vision for who you personally want to be will also breathe life into you. Writing it down will help you get there. If you want to learn a skill, get a degree, or become self-employed, write it down. I believe in having big, nearly impossible goals for myself, because if I come short of those goals I'll still be happy. If I create reasonable goals that are unimpressive and uninspiring, and they also fall short, it feels like a total loss. It almost would have been better not to have had a goal at all.

As mentioned earlier, as a personal discipline, I begin every single day writing down my goals on a legal pad. These are huge, crazy goals, first for my family and my relationship with God. Next, I write my goals for church and ministry. Finally, I write my professional and financial goals, along with personal goals for health and hobbies. I do this every single day and have done so for a long time. I also write a short one-sentence prayer and the number one thing I want to accomplish that day. Though this discipline sounds exhausting, I can tell you there is no better way to start the day. It's energizing. It gets me in the right mind-set, and it also helps me remember my priorities. It really only takes about half a page and three minutes to do.

If that's not for you, sometimes a good first step is to find one thing you want to develop. There's something great about having just one thing you're going to improve this year and focusing on that. The time when this happens for most people is in the New Year. Though New Year's resolutions are often criticized, I think they are great. Even when people don't achieve their resolutions (and most people don't), the process is still good. Again, anytime you have a dream or goal, it's good for your soul.

A Vision from Someone Who Loves You

Every year, Hannah and I make New Year's resolutions, but we put a twist on them. I pick her resolution, and she picks mine! Last year I resolved that she would read one nonfiction book every month. I know Hannah is always so busy giving to everyone, to me, to our kids, and to our church, that she rarely gets to pursue her own personal development. I thought this would not only help her but also give her the freedom to really go for personal growth. She did. Every month she picked some book on organizational leadership, psychology, theology, or another topic that interested her. I was shocked to see the last book was about tax accounting. It was so weird to see my artistic graphic-designer wife reading about tax law. But hey! It's what she wanted, and clearly, I could see pursuing personal growth was giving her life.

What did she pick for my New Year's resolution, you ask? Well, I'm sort of embarrassed to say she wanted me to serve more. I've never been the one to help with the dishes at family events or ask people if I can get them drinks. It's not that I'm opposed to it; I'm just oblivious. I talk a lot and am very extroverted. I lose my bearings and don't see the way others need help. So the challenge for me to serve more was also the challenge to notice. To notice the needs of visiting guests, to notice the basic needs of our kids (like lunch or changing diapers), and though she didn't mention it, to notice her needs too—to notice Hannah.

This last year I endeavored to improve in this one area. I've been helping with the kids in the morning, helping with cleaning around the house, and being more hospitable at home and at the office. I can say, without a doubt, Hannah has noticed, and it's meant the world to her, and I can say I feel sad that for so long I haven't been as attentive as I could have been to the needs of my friends and family.

Having one new big goal this year—"I'm going to serve others more and do it with joy"—has been such a great thing for me. I never would have picked it on my own, and I'm so glad to have discovered this shortcoming. Having a blind spot revealed can be painful or even embarrassing, but feeling like "I can change that thing" has been life giving and rewarding.

Perhaps your goal of personal growth has been to stop something. I find that those are the hardest: to stop smoking or lose weight (stop eating so much), for example. In those cases you are taking something away from your life. Perhaps if you've failed at those things in the past, you can make a different goal of personal growth for now and get a couple of wins under your belt. Perhaps you can dream about adding something to your life, like a new skill, class, or friendship. Then you will have the fortitude to go back to that thing later and try again with some new tools in your toolbox.[1] No matter what, personal goals and working on yourself are life giving. Never stop.

GREAT THINGS TAKE TIME

Whether your dream is as personal as "fixing my marriage" or as huge as "building a worldwide business," accomplishing your dreams takes time. If it were easy, everyone would do it. If it were quick, no one would give up. It means you have to be willing to do what most people won't. The best things take time to grow and are never without their bumps in the road. Every great vision, project, or dream requires

- enduring setbacks,
- evaluating those setbacks,
- tweaking the plan, and
- getting back to the vision.

This rhythm is common and predictable. Because of this, you can prepare and get your mind right. Setbacks are hard for morale, but they are an opportunity to improve the process. Everyone who has ultimately failed did so because they couldn't evaluate and endure the setback. You'll be different. It takes time and persistence, but you will get there. Don't give up on your dream in the eleventh hour.

Remember, to have the right kinds of thoughts you must be a dreamer. Dreams and visions nourish the soul. Don't let critics bring you down or break your heart. Realists are often right, but it's the dreamers who change the world.

--- *Training* ---

VERSE TO MEDITATE ON

"Where there is no vision, the people perish." (Prov. 29:18 kjv)

QUESTIONS TO CONSIDER

What would I attempt if I knew I couldn't fail? If I did
fail, what's the worst thing that would happen?

THOUGHT TO INHERIT

Defining a clear vision leads to fulfillment, joy, and achievement.

DISCIPLINE TO PRACTICE

One of the first steps to achievement is writing down your goals. This principle of having real and clearly defined goals has proven to be one of the greatest indicators of success. I write down my goals every day, and it has been a huge boon in my life. Try it for a week. Keep a legal pad and pen by your bed, and every morning write down all the big goals for your life.

First write your spiritual goals, then family and friendship goals, then financial, vocational, and physical goals. After that, write down the number one thing you want to accomplish that day and say a quick prayer over your life. This will dramatically keep your mind fixed on your values and vision for your life and ultimately will lead to greater success.

CHAPTER 7

REST AND INVEST IN YOU

We spend a lot of money in our culture on entertainment, but we spend very little money on the inner work of our self. That's an investment that ends up reaping benefits for the rest of your life.

—SARA BLAKELY

INVESTING IN YOU GIVES YOU FRESH VISION

Before my grandpa passed away, our family was blessed to have access to his apartment in Hawaii. He had acquired it back in the seventies for hardly anything, and he let my wife and I visit whenever we wanted. It was such a boon for us. Not only was it right on the water, but it was free! For the cost of a couple of plane tickets and some groceries, we could have a full-blown Hawaiian vacation. When we did, the most amazing thing happened. I came home with fresh vision.

We worked so hard in the ministry when we first planted our church. At the time we were not good at maintaining boundaries, and I would say yes to nearly everything. I preached every wedding and funeral. I was also the accountant for the church, the worship leader, the pastor, and the missions director. It felt as if the harder I worked, the less progress we made. I was trying to bring vision to our team and ministry but wasn't getting anywhere.

When we'd get to Hawaii, it would take days before I began to truly rest. When our plane landed, I'd rush to get the rental car, then groceries, maybe make some reservations at a restaurant or for beach activities. I'd feel antsy because I couldn't relax. I wanted to hurry up and rest!

Of course, after enough time my mind and body would relax

like a clenched fist opening up. I'd let go of needing to control the church and my life. I'd let go of needing to constantly jump when everyone needed me. Finally, I would gently fall into the easy rhythms of Hawaii. Soon, when I got to a place of total rest, I would be flooded with inspiration like a light from heaven. I had new ideas for ministry, new ideas for a sermon series, and I'd think of fresh ways we could make our church and life better. I'd recognize all that was good about life in those moments of rest.

BURNING THE CANDLE AT BOTH ENDS IS NO WAY TO LIVE A GOOD LIFE.

Every trip to Hawaii was like that. By the third trip or so, I realized that something needed to change in my life. I didn't need to go to Hawaii to have fresh vision. I needed boundaries. I needed rest. I needed to invest in myself, because only then would I be effective in investing in others. Burning the candle at both ends is no way to live a good life.

Your future begins in your thinking. Your career, your happiness, your family, and anything else you want begins with what you think about today. Good thoughts and good thinking will always lead to a good future. When our minds are stretching and growing, the future will be bright. But consider this: growing toward your future requires that you rest and invest.

SABBATH REST

Many of us feel exhausted. After several days in a row of working, attending events, and caring for the needs of others, we don't have enough energy to pick up a book, attend a cooking class, or participate in another activity we've been longing to do. After pouring out all day, it may feel like there is nothing left for ourselves. When the day is done, it's all we can do to sit back and browse our phones or watch television to unwind before going to bed.

This is not God's best for our lives. Though it's the most common way people are living, God has something better in store for us: personal growth—one of the main functions of Sabbath. God wants us to personally grow because growing things are living things. We feel most alive when we are growing. Though stress, challenges, and service to others will certainly cause us to grow in some capacity, these are limited in their ability to help us reach our full potential. For growth, living things require rest.

REST ISN'T A LUXURY, IT'S A NECESSITY

I learned this recently when I was trying to build some body muscle to look better and feel stronger. When I was researching workouts and diet plans, I was surprised to find the most common mistake new weight lifters make is over-working: working out too much, not taking breaks, or not getting adequate amounts of sleep.

This is because when athletes train with weights or other equipment, they are creating the catalyst for growth—stress on the body. But the actual growing happens *when the muscles are at rest*. In other words, muscles need both stress and rest to grow. Without rest, injury is bound to occur, at which point growth will decrease. When someone wants to grow as an athlete, he or she must catalyze the body for growth through stress, then allow growth through rest.

This principle also applies to a growing mind and soul. The stress of caring for our children, friends, and community is good for us; it is the stimulus for personal growth. But if most of our time is spent doing that, we will run out of gas and have nothing left to give. Our service to others will become an act of sheer willpower rather than a work of love coming from a full heart. If all you do is serve others and never rest, play, and grow personally, you will not be a help to anyone any longer. You will become a self-pitying martyr. That's no good for anyone. You deserve some rest.

BREATHE

Living in the power of the Holy Spirit is like breathing. We must inhale and exhale, a rhythm like the ocean lapping the shore. The word for *spirit* in the Bible also means "breath." The work we do—caring for others, ministering, giving—is like exhaling. But learning, resting, and praying is like inhaling. Both are equally important and vital, yet in most churches almost all the value is put on the stuff going out, not going in. Too often we try to exhale when we haven't inhaled in a long time. Our lungs are empty, and we have nothing to give. Taking time for yourself to reflect, relax, learn, and have fun is fundamental to living a godly life.

When we fly commercially, the flight attendant tells us that in case of an emergency, oxygen masks will fall from the ceiling. We are reminded that adults must put their masks on before putting the masks on children. Otherwise, the lack of oxygen may result in an incapacitated adult, unable to assist those who are weaker or less able to help themselves. Apply this same principle to your life. You can't help other people if you are suffocating. Invest in you. You're worth it.

INVESTING IN YOU HELPS RELATIONSHIPS

My wife, Hannah, said to me once, "Investing in *you* is one of the best ways you can invest in others." She's right: investing in yourself will result in you having more energy, which allows your relationships to flourish. Whether it is taking time for yourself to do something you love or growing by enrolling in a class, growing as a person allows you to be a better help to those who need you.

When you invest in yourself through rest, retreat, solitude, and silence, you bring something meaningful from the quiet places of your life. For example, if I'm stressed and hurried, I come to hurting people trying to quickly produce effective results in the shortest time possible. Ironically, this is the worst thing I can do. But when I'm living from a place of rest, it's easier for me to listen without hurrying or trying to manufacture results in their lives. I can be the quiet, loving presence they need.

INVESTING IN YOU IS GOOD STEWARDSHIP

Though many of us grind away in exhausting jobs, some of us working sixty to eighty hours a week, this is not the best way to build wealth. However, if you invest in yourself to learn more and to bring, as Warren Buffett's multibillionaire investment partner Charlie Munger puts it, a "multi-disciplinary" perspective to work and investing, it will pay off.[1] That is, you become better at your job and your investments when you understand more subjects that affect those jobs and investments. Having informed opinions rather than being emotional and "hopeful" about a financial decision is key to succeeding. This happens by doing things like reading books, seeking mentors, and listening to podcasts not limited to just the task at hand. Learning Spanish or Arabic may make you more versatile in your engineering job. Experimenting with art will make you a more creative parent. Studying the Bible, especially the Proverbs, will make you a better accountant. Munger would say that having a cursory knowledge of topics like psychology and physics will give you a distinct advantage in nearly every vocation and investment. In other words, though it may seem trivial or a waste of time, learning any discipline is always a good financial decision.

One of the greatest psychological roadblocks to people learning and growing is a misunderstanding about resources. People think, *If I had more time, I'd invest in me. But I have to work all the time to make money to pay the bills.* The truth is, not learning, growing, or resting will cause you to lose out on opportunities.

Once, coming home on a plane, I was intrigued by a magazine article titled "Shark Tank Stars Mark Cuban and Sara Blakely Tell Us How They Got to Their First $1 Million—And How You Can, Too." The article featured a double interview with Mark Cuban, the business titan owner of the Dallas Mavericks, and Sara Blakely, the founder of the global company Spanx. They were both notably young when they crossed that "three-comma line" to become billionaires. At first they gave the same rote advice everyone gives to become a millionaire:

"Don't spend more than you make."

"Don't get into debt unless it's for an investment."

"Diversify!"

But when the topic of investing in yourself came up, they lit up. It clearly seemed like this was the number one bit of advice they could give:

Sara Blakely: When you do spend money, think about what you are spending it on and what the return is. For my particular journey, I spent money on motivational and inspirational tapes, and all of my friends made fun of me and laughed at me.

Mark Cuban: I did the same thing. I did the same thing.

Sara Blakely: Right! I was spending money investing in myself. Just like an athlete: You can have two athletes that have the same kind of physical strength, but why does one win? It's mental. It's always mental. Never underestimate the power of your brain, and that's your greatest asset.

Mark Cuban: So true.

Sara Blakely: We spend a lot of money in our culture on entertainment, but we spend very little money on the inner work of our self. That's an investment that ends up reaping benefits for the rest of your life.

Mark Cuban: I used to ride around all day looking at big houses, listening to Zig Ziglar on motivational tapes that I bought for half price at Half Price Books. Absolutely.[2]

This is something you will hear a lot when you look at people who are successful in any area of life. They take time to learn and grow. They know that investing in themselves is the best investment they can make. As Blakely said, "Never underestimate the power of your brain, and that's your greatest asset."

CLEAR EYES

As my friend Dave Martin has said, "Tired eyes can't see a bright future."[3] People are so afraid of losing their jobs, for example. But I find when hard workers lose their jobs, they almost always end up with a major upgrade, a better job. That's because, in the time of rest while they're looking for new work, they are able to get fresh eyes and a fresh vision for all the opportunities they missed while they were grinding away at their previous jobs. Tired eyes can't see a bright future, but relaxed, clear eyes can see a world of possibility. Take time to relax, lots of time. It's one of the best ways to be more productive. So:

- If you want to connect better with people, take time to disconnect.
- If you want to make more money, take time to learn.
- If you want to be more productive, take time to relax.

Of course, this sounds similar to the upside-down kingdom principles Jesus uses in his sermons and parables:

- He who wants to gain his life must lose it (Luke 17:33).
- He who humbles himself will be exalted (Matt. 23:12).
- He who gives will receive (Matt. 6:2).
- And, of course, the Sabbath principle: Even God rested; so should we (Ex. 20:11).

INVESTING IN YOU BRINGS SUCCESS

Rest is a gift from God that you may not be receiving. With a relaxed and joyful mind, we can accomplish so much more. I believe that's one reason honoring the Sabbath gets placed by God squarely in the Ten Commandments with others like "Do not murder" and "Do not steal." It's that important to God. In fact, honoring the Sabbath is the most repeated moral command in the Bible. Here's why:

Sabbath teaches us that although our work, ministry, and finances are important, our power to do well in those things does not come from us; it comes from God. When we leave this world, our work, ministry, economy, and everything else will carry on without us because God will carry it on. When we learn to Sabbath well, we learn to do everything else well.

> SABBATH TEACHES US THAT ALTHOUGH OUR WORK, MINISTRY, AND FINANCES ARE IMPORTANT, OUR POWER TO DO WELL IN THOSE THINGS DOES NOT COME FROM US; IT COMES FROM GOD.

A Sabbath mind is not just the mind of a person who honors Sabbath one day a week. Rather, it's the principle that work comes from rest, that good results come from thinking, and that a life without joy is not one worth living. Think about it like this: in the Jewish worldview, a day begins at sundown, not sunrise. So the Sabbath day itself begins on Friday night at sundown and ends Saturday at sundown.

- First dark, then light.
- First sleep, then wake.
- First rest, then work.

This is because the brightest light comes out of the darkness, the most energy comes after a good night's sleep, and the best and most imaginative work comes from thinking and resting.

Christians used to care deeply about the Sabbath, enough so that entire denominations sprang up based on which day it should be honored. Today many Christians just can't seem to find the time for Sabbath rest at all. But for those few who still understand its unbelievable capacity to create a moral society, as well as create personal joy, growth, and wealth, Sabbath is still a priority.

For Christians, Sabbath typically occurs on Sunday—the first day of the week. Most people forget that. Most people think Monday is the first day of the week, but it's not. This "Monday view" of life says Monday is the first (and worst) day of the week. It's the day we have to trudge off to work, tired and disappointed. Then on Friday, the best day of the week, we get to go home excited to get a break. Everyone works hard for five days to earn a two-day reward. Unfortunately, most people are let down by the weekend because they don't get what they hoped they would get (true rest and a serene mind), and as Sunday afternoon begins to rear its ugly head, a sense of dread sets in that says, *Oh man, I've got to go back to work tomorrow.*

The "Sabbath view" of the week is different. On Sunday, the first day of the week, I begin with rest. I gather with my friends at church, where I'm going to pray, play, and learn. Any great church does these three things well. After that, the rest of the day I'm going to connect deeply with my family or friends. I'm going to truly rest by doing what I love: reading a favorite book, enjoying my hobbies, and letting go of my need to produce. Then, going into the workweek, I bring a relaxed mind, full of joy and fresh ideas. I see my work as a mission field. I look for opportunities and ways I can improve through my work, and I grow.

A Sabbath mind is one that takes time to rest, pray, play, and learn. It's the kind of mentality that says, *Investing in me God's way is one of the smartest things I can do. I will make that a priority.* Sabbath is not lazy; it's amazingly productive. Investing in you is not selfish; it is godly.

MOST PROBLEMS ARE KNOWLEDGE PROBLEMS

What if we saw every problem we faced as a knowledge problem? There's a way to be a better spouse or parent, if only we can learn it. There's a way out of our money problems; we just need to learn it. There's a cure for cancer; we just haven't discovered it. Most problems have knowledge solutions that can be found in a book, from a mentor, or through experience. Knowledge truly is power.

All knowledge is good and valuable and will benefit you in the long run. Attaining knowledge is never a waste of time or effort. So invest in you by learning.

- Learn a language.
- Take a class or seminar on something that interests you.
- Excel at your favorite hobby.
- Read a nonfiction book every month.

If you want to take a cooking class, learn to fly or sail, take a dance class, or study martial arts, do it! Make time to do it. You will feel more alive and joyful because you will be growing. Even if you get into it and decide to bow out, you will be glad you took a step toward personal growth. You never know if your desire to learn a language is actually a part of God's calling for your life. God uses everything, even things as simple as fishing, cooking, or basketball, to get people to their destinies. So don't feel guilty for investing in you. It's one of the smartest investments you can make.

People need you, and they need a lot from you. If you invest only in others and never invest in yourself, you will not be able to meet anyone's needs, especially not your own. You will begin to resent people and will regret that you haven't personally grown in a while. But if you invest in yourself by learning, resting, and playing, you will have a full tank to help others. They need a joyful you, and that will only come if you take time for yourself and your personal growth.

Take time for you—time to grow and time to rest. Invest in yourself. You're worth it. That kind of thinking will not only help you achieve more, but it will also help you lead others toward more meaningful life.

Training

VERSE TO MEDITATE ON

"It is a sign between me and the Israelites forever, for in six days the LORD made the heavens and the earth, and on the seventh day he rested and was refreshed." (Ex. 31:17)

QUESTIONS TO CONSIDER

If I had an extra day off every week, only for me, what would I do on that day? If I could learn something new, what would I pursue?

THOUGHT TO INHERIT

Investing in myself is one of the best ways to invest in the people I love.

DISCIPLINE TO PRACTICE

Practice the Sabbath and do it well. If you can't get a Sunday off, most churches offer services on other days of the week. If your kids are in sports programs on Sunday, consider pulling them from the program or changing sports. When you choose sports over church, you are sending a clear message to your kids about your values.

On Sunday don't just go to church. Make the whole day a day of real rest. Eat well if you can. If you're married, talk to your spouse about having an hour or two to yourself to have a small retreat. Offer to give them one as well. Read or pray and get ready for Monday. Whatever you do, make time for yourself. Put it on your calendar, and be intentional not to watch TV or fool around on the internet, but instead to grow in a hobby or intellectual discipline.

CHAPTER 8

GOD LOVES MY BODY

God has given us our bodies,
and our mental capabilities
define its limitations.

—SAMIR SINGH

THOUGHT TO INHERIT: *My body is a gift, even though it's imperfect.*

Have you ever slept in when you shouldn't have or eaten a piece of chocolate cake you swore you wouldn't eat? Have you ever skipped your exercise class over and over until you finally had to quit your membership because you were wasting money?

King Solomon, author of Proverbs, reminded readers that wisdom is a source of physical health. He said:

> My son, pay attention to what I say;
>> turn your ear to my words.
> Do not let them out of your sight,
>> keep them within your heart;
> for they are life to those who find them
>> and health to one's whole body. (Prov. 4:20–22)

Healthier thinking leads to a healthier body.

If you love your body, it will love you back. If you hate your body, it will only give you more trouble. Most people have little things about their bodies they dislike. We have scars, stretch marks, fat, not enough muscle, and imperfections on our skin or face that make us feel unattractive. On top of that, our bodies get sick. Even if you have a flawless body in every way imaginable, time will take its toll. You will get wrinkles, your hair will thin and gray, and many other changes will take place with aging.

It doesn't help that only the most touched-up, beautiful bodies are shown in the media. Those bodies have expertly applied makeup, professionally done hair, and special lighting, and often the models or stars have employed extreme diets to appear perfect for that one shoot. Even then the photos are touched up to make them even more "perfect." Though we know this full well, we can't help but compare ourselves to these idealized beauties and find ourselves lacking.

The thing is, your body is amazing and a real gift from God to you. You won't have it forever, so treat it with compassion. Love your body because God loves it too. The apostle Paul told the church in Corinth, "Do you not know that your bodies are temples of the Holy Spirit, who is in you, whom you have received from God? You are not your own; you were bought at a price. Therefore honor God with your bodies" (1 Cor. 6:19–20). Someday God will give us new heavenly bodies that will be better than the ones we have now. But that doesn't mean these bodies aren't a gift and aren't sacred to him.

YOUR BODY IS YOUR FRIEND

A friend of mine had a near-death experience, but she said she wasn't afraid at all. She stood over her dead body, looking at it as though she were saying goodbye to an old friend. That story touched me, because I started to think about all the ways I've inadvertently done harm to my body, treated it with contempt, or at times even hated it.

Because our bodies are directly related to our minds, this is a key area in which we need to change our thinking. God loves your body. You should too. Say and think good things about your body. The more you do, the healthier and happier you will be.

Whether we want to quit smoking or drinking, lose weight,

exercise more, or sleep better, we all intuitively understand that being healthy is, in part, a battle of the wits. It's not enough to wake up inspired on some morning early in January and declare, "I'm getting in shape!" Rather, months later, when kids, work, and life have taken so much of our time and energy, we still need to make time for exercise. For most people, losing weight is not about knowing how to lose weight. We all know about carbs and calories. We need willpower and consistency to change our habits.

In other words, physical health has everything to do with what's going on in your mind. Though we all have genetic advantages or disadvantages, those who have the will and mental control are the ones able to accomplish their goals for a healthier body.

In turn, a healthier body will lead to a healthier mind and life. It's a feedback loop. When we feel good physically, we think well about ourselves, our outlook improves, and it's easier to deal with the difficulties of life and difficult people in general. When we have the flu, for example, the exact opposite happens. We aren't dreaming, we are not able to help others, and we aren't thinking right. Therefore, a healthy mind leads to a healthier body and life, which in turn leads to a healthier mind, and so on.

Of course, no matter how old or young you are, no matter if you have the body of an Olympian, or if you have a limiting disability, you can always be healthier than you are now. By changing the way you think, you can have a healthier body six months from now than you do today.

Even if you are extraordinarily fit and have reached all your physical goals, you still may be in danger of other harm to your body that comes from things like stress, chronic anxiety, and isolation, factors that can have a bigger impact on your longevity than smoking or being overweight. There are many examples of this, but one of my favorites is in a book about community by John Ortberg:

> One of the most thorough research projects on relationships is called the Alameda County Study. Headed by a Harvard social scientist, it tracked the lives of 7,000 people over nine years. Researchers found that the most isolated people were *three times more likely to die* than those with strong relational connections.
>
> People who had bad health habits (such as smoking, poor eating habits, obesity, or alcohol use) but strong social ties lived *significantly longer* than people who had great health habits but were isolated. In other words, it is better to eat Twinkies with good friends than to eat broccoli alone.[1]

The positive effects of community in particular on our thinking and perspectives are more beneficial for our physical health than even losing weight. This only reinforces the point: a healthy body begins with a mind that is in line with healthy thoughts. When we are connecting deeply with God and others, our bodies get healthier. When we stop worrying and abandon our outcomes to God, often our bodies will get healthier. When we learn the true God-given power within, we can accomplish our physical goals.

STRENGTH ORIGINATES IN THE IMAGINATION

If you're fighting addiction, training for a marathon, or just trying to sleep better, your strength is in your mind. If you have a strong mind, you'll have a stronger body. In a clever way, this is what Jesus taught his disciples during a famous encounter he had with other religious teachers.

First, some context: In Jesus' day, a new system of teaching Scripture was emerging, often referred to as "rabbinic Judaism." This system began with the idea that the Torah, the Jewish Bible, had to be deeply engrained in its people. A school system was created in which all Jewish children were required to memorize the Torah. By elementary school age, children would know the entire Torah cover to cover.

Within the Torah, in Deuteronomy 6:4, is a holy prayer known by every Jew called the *Shema*, a word that means "hear!" The Shema goes like this: "Hear, O Israel, the LORD our God, the LORD is one."

This verse constitutes probably the most important Bible verse for first-century Jews. Even today, if you visit a Jewish friend's home, you will likely see a tiny box attached to the entryway called a mezuzah. In this little box is a scroll with this same verse.

Just after this verse, Deuteronomy 6:5 says, "Love the LORD your God with all your *heart*, and with all your *soul*, and with all your *strength*" (emphasis added).

With all your heart, soul, and strength.

1. Heart
2. Soul
3. Strength

Remember these three words.

Every Jew alive, male or female, as long as they were older than five years old, would absolutely know this verse.

In Matthew 22:34–40, Jesus was being questioned by the religious leaders of his day. Many admired him but others hated him, so it's likely they were trying to rhetorically trap him when they asked, "Teacher, which is the greatest commandment in the Law?" Here, when they said "the Law," it can mean any part of the Torah, but more than likely they meant the Ten Commandments. The trap here was, if Jesus responded with "Do not murder," for example, they would have something about which they could argue.

Instead, Jesus answered with the verse everyone would know, but he changed one word. He said, "Love the Lord your God with all your heart, and with all your soul, and with all your *mind*." Did you catch that? Everyone listening would have. It would be as if I said in a prayer, "Thy kingdom come, thy will be done, in Los Angeles as it is in heaven." Everyone would get it. He changed the word "strength" to the word "mind." In doing so, he made a beautiful rhetorical point about the mind. He was saying, "Your strength is in your mind." In the eyes of Rabbi Jesus, loving God with your strength is the same as loving him with your mind.

The strength to do what you need to do begins in your mind. A strong mind leads to a stronger body. A weak mind leads to a weaker body. If you have a strong body, it's because you had the kind of thinking that made it so. If you have a healthy body, it's because you have had healthy thoughts to get you there. Strength in every aspect of your life begins first with your thinking.

One of my favorite stories that proves this point is about Samir Singh, the so-called "Faith Runner." Singh has broken several records for long-distance running and continues to show that if you believe it can be done, your belief becomes your reality. I heard of him for the first time in the summer of 2017. My wife and I were driving to the airport and heard on the radio a story about a man who nearly ran 10,000 kilometers in 100 days but fell short by only 36 kilometers. At the age of forty-four, Singh had run one hundred kilometers for one hundred days straight, except on the last and final day; so close to the finish line, he fell short and collapsed. Though barely incomplete, this achievement blew the minds of all who were watching.

THE STRENGTH TO DO WHAT YOU NEED TO DO BEGINS IN YOUR MIND.

"People say the body has limits," Singh, who is also a coach, said. "My students have complained of being advised against over using their bodies. But according to the holy scriptures, the body has no limit. If you have dreams your body will take shape accordingly. My experience is testament to the same. God has given us our bodies and our mental capabilities define its limitations."[2] To be fair, here he was referring to the god of his own Hindu faith and scriptures. Because I don't endorse Hinduism, I'm uncomfortable even mentioning it, but I believe this is actually true about Yahweh God. God loves our bodies and has made them with almost limitless abilities. Singh understands this. He understands that the body, for the most part, is fueled by our thinking.

He proved the point twice. The first in breaking, as a forty-four-year-old, our understanding of how long and far the human body can run. But he proved the point a second time in coming just short and collapsing. When Hannah and I heard this part of the story, we both thought the same thing. We wondered if in the end he lost the mental game. Hannah said to me, "If only someone had tricked him into thinking it was day 99 instead of day 100."

SANCTIFY THE IMAGINATION

The kind of healthy mind that leads to a healthier body is one in which the imagination is sanctified. We must imagine what it would be like to be healthy, even when we are sick, overweight, not sleeping well, or feeling old. Rather than dwelling on what we don't like, we begin to imagine what it would be like to be healthier.

The imagination is a good thing. I remember once a friend of mine criticized my faith, saying, "Bobby, this God thing is all your imagination." I said, "Yes, that's true, in part!" Just because we imagine something doesn't mean it isn't real. I must imagine God, not because he doesn't exist, but because he is invisible and sometimes feels far away. In the same way, I imagined being married when I was single. I'm glad Hannah exists. Before I traveled to Holland for the first time, I imagined what it was like, and in many ways it was true.

The imagination is where everything created begins. Disneyland exists because Walt Disney dreamed it up. Just laws begin in the imagination. So does the breaking of those laws. Every building, business, and invention began in the imagination. So did nearly every war crime, theft, and infidelity. This is why we must sanctify our imaginations. We must "take captive every thought to make it obedient to Christ" (2 Cor. 10:5), as the apostle Paul said.

DREAM

Our imaginations only have so much bandwidth. This is why dreaming is so important. Even if you rarely accomplish your dreams, dreaming is still healthy because it keeps your mind fixed on things that are positive rather than things that can lead to despair, anxiety, and fear. The more I dream about my future, what I could accomplish or who I could be for God and his purpose, the less I worry about what could go wrong. The more I fixate on what could go wrong in my life, the less likely I am to dream or do something great. With our bodies, fixating on what is bad will likely make the situation worse, but churning up hopes and dreams by imagining what it would be like to be healthier will likely make things better. It can even lead to a full recovery.

HEALING

Dodie Osteen beat cancer by simply getting her thoughts right. In the 1980s she was told she had terminal cancer and would only have a few months to live, but she decided she wouldn't give up that easily. When she would fall into moments of despair, she would say, "Thoughts, get in line with the Word of God!" She wrote down scriptures that had to do with healing and physical health and placed them around her house as reminders that God's Word is the last word. In this way she was sanctifying her imagination. She received a miracle from God by aligning her thoughts with his Word and is still alive nearly thirty years later, proclaiming that God can still heal.

For Dodie it all began in the mind. She would say this doesn't work for everybody, but it certainly can't hurt. If you give up in your mind, how do you expect your body to recover?

To receive healing, we must believe we can be healed. Yes, sometimes people aren't healed and it's their time, but Dodie simply believed it wasn't her time. She did not want to die just because she lacked the faith to get better. There is no magic formula and God is sovereign, but God still does miracles today just as he did in the stories in the Bible.

What you imagine shapes your future. Imagine being

healthier. What you dwell on becomes your reality. When we imagine all the terrible things that could happen to us, we recede into a life geared toward safety and never do anything brave. When we imagine getting back at the people who hurt us, bitterness gets into our language and into our bodies. We become angrier and more defensive. But when we imagine raising godly children, having an amazing marriage, or building a great business or ministry, a different future takes shape. When we imagine being healthy despite how we look or feel now, we build a dream in our hearts that will give us the willpower to push through the challenges in the way.

WHAT YOU BELIEVE MATTERS

Even without a belief in God, your imagination can cure you. Scientists call it the placebo effect. With every test done for a new medication, the scientific method requires that a control group be used. This group is given a substance with no effect, such as a sugar pill, and is told it's the new treatment. The reason they do this is because sometimes up to 30 percent of those taking the placebo will see dramatic improvements, even cures, despite the fact that nothing has actually changed. The only change is their thoughts. Because they believe the medicine is a cure, it becomes so.

WHAT YOU DWELL ON BECOMES YOUR REALITY.

The healthy mind leads to a healthy life. If you imagine you are getting sick, you are more likely to get sick. If you see the worst in your body, you'll start getting the worst. If you imagine you are getting better, you are more likely to improve. Shouldn't we focus on what we dwell on and do our best to think the kinds of thoughts that will bring us into greater health?

Think healthy thoughts. Don't dwell on things that are dark. Don't watch movies or listen to music that shapes your imagination in a negative way. I don't recommend horror movies, for example, especially when they incorporate demonic images and themes. Even if you think they're fun, it's not worth the way those mediums shape the way you think. Many people who saw *The Exorcist* regret it.

Rather, read biographies of everyday people who have done great things. Take long breaks to pray, relax, and fix your mind on God. Listen to music that inspires you, makes you feel thoughtful or calm. These little changes are good for your body. Just remember, you decide every day how you will train your mind by consuming things that are healthy or harmful.

You won't eat better, sleep better, kick your bad habits, or go to the gym consistently unless you get your mind right. This is because you have more power over what you think about than you have over what you do. Your actions are merely the result of your pattern of thinking.

RECEIVE THE LOVE GOD HAS FOR YOUR WHOLE SELF

God loves your body. It's a temporary gift to you and a sanctuary of the Holy Spirit. Think better of your body, the way you look in particular. Observe how thinking good thoughts about your body dramatically affects your overall mood and experience of life in general. Don't feel shame; rather, practice gratitude. Thank God for giving you a body unique to you. Such thoughts can lead to a healthier life.

VERSE TO MEDITATE ON

"Do you not know that your bodies are temples of the Holy
Spirit, who is in you, whom you have received from God?
You are not your own; you were bought at a price. Therefore
honor God with your bodies." (1 Cor. 6:19–20)

QUESTION TO CONSIDER

What's something about my body or appearance that I appreciate?

THOUGHT TO INHERIT

My body is a gift even though it's imperfect.

DISCIPLINE TO PRACTICE

Forgive your body.

Once when I was preparing a message on forgiveness, I felt the Holy
Spirit strongly say to me, "Tell them to forgive their bodies." I was meditating on how the Scriptures show forgiveness leading the way to healing.
But very often we will become angry with our bodies, as though we resent
them. *It's not doing what it's supposed to do*, we may think. Though it may
sound weird, one way to have a kinder view of your body is to forgive it.
Watch how praying for your body in a spirit of forgiveness can be the first
step to healing.

CHAPTER 9

FROM OBSTACLES TO OPPORTUNITY

The impediment to action
advances the action. What stands
in the way becomes the way.

—ATTRIBUTED TO ROMAN
EMPEROR MARCUS AURELIUS

THOUGHT TO INHERIT: *Every loss and challenge can be a doorway to a better version of me.*

In college, I had an amazing opportunity to live briefly in Germany. I received a call from one of my Grandpa Schuller's friends, David, who owned a television network in Canada. He asked if I'd like to be an intern and do some hosting work at their new studio in Germany. The World's Fair had just begun, and they were recruiting a handful of young people to host a new show, *Frequency X*, which would cover the various pavilions at the fair as well as the rock concerts coming through. He was basically asking me to host an MTV-style show and experience every national culture on earth while meeting famous people and bands for free. I couldn't say yes quick enough. Little did I know how much I would hate it and suffer the first few months I was there.

In short, I was bad at the job. I don't know if you've ever had to talk in front of a camera when thousands (or even millions) of people are going to see you, but it changes you somehow. It's hard to explain the surreal experience of talking to a lens instead of a person, how simultaneously embarrassed and nervous you feel, especially when you have to watch it later. This was amplified by the fact I had pretty bad acne that seemed to be magnified on camera.

I would stand there holding a microphone as if I were a newscaster interviewing some important person or group of people standing around me, and I would forget my line, mess up a name, or freeze entirely. Once I did more than thirty takes of a simple paragraph, and the crew was so frustrated they took a lunch break. I was dying on the inside, felt like a complete failure, and desperately wanted to go home. And that was the first month. Only five months left to go.

The great thing about the trip was that I wasn't allowed to quit. Though I was homesick and felt like a total failure, they needed me. We had a deal. I had agreed to do it. And so over time I got more comfortable. Some of the guys on the team coached me, and I did a better job of preparing beforehand. By the end, I was actually okay, even good at times. Though the job was incredibly humiliating, painful, and arduous, I gained a rare skill I had no idea I would use later in life.

About six years later, I was in seminary preparing to become a pastor. I was invited to be a judge on a new television program called *The Messengers*. This was big. Not only did it pay well, it was poised to be TLC's biggest show. The goal was to "find America's next inspirational speaker." They invested in media training and expensive top-level interview training for the cast. The hopes were remarkably high. People were saying this was going to be the next *American Idol*. One of the contestants even got a *The Messenger* tattoo on his arm. I didn't blame him. If only you could feel what we were feeling.

Have you ever heard of the big TV show *The Messengers*? That's what I thought. Most people haven't. It wasn't a total flop. The show was actually quite good from a quality standpoint, and it rated okay but not great. Unfortunately, it aired in 2008, just when the global economy was collapsing. When the season ended it was discontinued, and none of us got to carry on our dream of being highly influential TV personas. It felt like a personal failure and a tremendous disappointment. I thought for sure my life on television was over. Good riddance.

Years after that, I was pastoring a church plant in Orange, California, when the *Hour of Power* board invited me to guest preach at the now bankrupt Crystal Cathedral. Though the church was going to leave the iconic cathedral and there was no money left in the bank, the cameras were still on and the leaders were committed to bringing a message of hope to people around the world, even if it was for just a few more weeks.

Now, for many young and inexperienced pastors, getting in front of those cameras to preach would have been very difficult. They would have forgotten their lines, messed up names and prayers, or frozen entirely. But I didn't. It wasn't that I was gifted in some way; it was that I'd already been through the crucible. I had been through months of arduous training on how to talk into a camera and be relaxed. You see, all those years ago back in Germany, when I felt like a failure and wondered why I would be so stupid to take such a difficult job without any experience, I had no idea that the pain was a part of my preparation for this day. That morning, standing before the cameras was easy, even fun. The rest is history.

When people say, "You're so natural in front of the camera," they think it's some kind of talent that runs in my family or something. Little do they know I used to be the worst. God used what I thought were two huge embarrassing failures, Germany and *The Messengers*, to prepare me for my destiny.

Maybe you're going through the crucible now. Maybe you just got through it and you feel like it was one big waste of time, a total failure. I assure you, the last chapter has not been written on your life. If you give your past to God, he will carry you to a bright future. Throughout life, the challenges, obstacles, and suffering we experience can become the very doorways that lead us to our destinies.

Within every setback is an opportunity. In his amazing book *The Obstacle Is the Way*, Ryan Holiday opens with a quote from the famous Roman emperor and philosopher-king Marcus Aurelius. His famous line has fueled some of the most successful people in history. He said, "The impediment to action advances the action. What stands in the way becomes the way." The idea is that in every tragedy, hardship, and setback there's an amazing opportunity most people miss. Within the loss is another kind of gain. Holiday shows the reader that in every challenge in life is a deeper gift. He asks, "What if embedded inside it or inherent in [every problem] were certain benefits—benefits only for you?"[1] He says life is often like the Chinese story about the king who blocked the way to the city.

It goes like this: Once there was a king who became frustrated with the people in his city. He could see they were becoming lazy and complacent in life. So, to teach them a deeper lesson about living, he blocked the entrance to the city with a huge boulder. Hiding in the bushes, he looked on to see how his people would respond. Some came and cursed the rock. Others cursed the king. Still others, when seeing it, simply turned around and went the other way.

Finally, a poor man came and, seeing the rock, tried to move it. He pushed and pried to no avail. Eventually he went into the woods to find a large branch that would work as a lever. After toiling and finally moving the massive boulder, the gate opened once again and people were free to go in and out of the city. But even more important, lying there in the rut where the boulder once stood was a bag of gold and a letter from the king: "The obstacle to the path becomes the path. Never forget that in every obstacle is an opportunity to improve our condition." This sounds like Marcus Aurelius, doesn't it? "The impediment to the action advances the action. What stands in the way becomes the way." What if, within every challenge in life, every heart-wrenching, morale-killing blow, there's actually a hidden gift we will attain at the other side? What if every time we decide to move the boulder blocking the gate, we don't just get an open gate but discover a bag of gold?

When we face setbacks in life, our temptation will be to curse them, dwell on self-pity, blame others, or hurry on to something that isn't meant to be. But a big part of the journey of a disciple of Jesus is to wait in hopeful expectation, to see the world through the Easter lens. That is, we are to believe that no matter how bad a thing is, Christ has the power to transform it to even greater life. There is no tragedy God can't redeem. Though you cannot see it now, God will get you through whatever it is you're facing, and you might even find a gift within.

> WE ARE TO BELIEVE THAT NO MATTER HOW BAD A THING IS, CHRIST HAS THE POWER TO TRANSFORM IT TO EVEN GREATER LIFE. THERE IS NO TRAGEDY GOD CAN'T REDEEM.

When it comes to the greatest tragedy in life, such as the death of a loved one, Christ has provided a way out of the grief. We can be sure that those who knew the Lord are safe with him. Dying is much more like waking up than falling asleep. Christ has taken their death and combined it with his own so they can receive life in heaven. But that still doesn't change the fact that you feel brokenhearted, lost, or abandoned by God. How could he take away your spouse or your good friend? How are you supposed to get through that kind of a challenge?

When tragedies like this happen, our temptation is to withdraw, to try and just forget about it. Sometimes the temptation is to act happy, even though inside we are hurting and brokenhearted. It's easy to feel like other friends or family members are trying to hurry us through the process, to get us to the other side quickly. Though they just want the best for us, they don't understand that hurrying through the pain only makes it last longer. They don't know that the best way to get through the pain of loss is to dive deeper into it, to talk about the pain of the loss, and to ask how God can use the loss to somehow bring a transformation to you.

We can't control what happens in life. Things like your house burning down, your partner cheating on you, or being sued unfairly—these are unpredictable and can hit without warning. They can feel like real deaths. We may wonder, *How am I going to recover from this one? How will I ever get back?* The answer is, maybe you're not supposed to "get back." Maybe the setback is a setup for the next chapter in your story.

Viktor Frankl taught us that, though we cannot control what happens in life, we can control how we respond. We can't keep people from harming us or prevent all accidents from happening. We can't do much when governments or our places of work pass policies that hinder or even harm us. But we can decide how to respond. We can get bitter and angry. We can dwell on the past and get poisoned with regret and frustration. We can look to the future negatively and wonder, *What does this all mean? How are things going to be from here on out? Will it always be like this?* Or we can find meaning, somehow, within the darkness of the loss itself. We can allow it to change us in a positive way. We can ask that God would use this death to bring new life.

This is called the "paschal mystery." Jesus taught, "Unless a kernel of wheat falls to the ground and dies, it remains only a single seed. But if it dies, it produces many seeds" (John 12:24). What he meant was, God loves to take what the enemy meant for bad and turn it to good. He loves to turn tragedies into triumphs. When death, tragedy, or loss strikes someone who believes in Christ, it transforms them into something greater, which opens a world of new possibilities.

My grandfather Dr. Schuller said, "Anyone can count the seeds in an apple, but only God can count the apples in a seed." Within you there is so much life, potential, and power. But, like a seed, the difficulties you think are so awful are sometimes the very thing that unlocks virtue, courage, growth, and fresh vision in your life. You may not see it today, but the pain you are going through may be the very thing that ultimately gets you to your destiny. God uses what the enemy means for bad and turns it to our greater victory.

So how does that happen? How can we change our thoughts when it comes to tragedy and difficulty? The answer is this: when we can't change something bad in our lives, we ask God to use it to change us. In this way, the obstacle becomes the path. The challenge becomes the doorway. And within the big loss, we find an even bigger gift.

The average person will likely endure something like five to ten major tragedies in his or her lifetime, tragedies like the death of a loved one. Then there are other sufferings, the smaller un-expected and unplanned tragedies we also face in life, like losing a job or having our credit stolen. How do we apply the Easter prin-ciple when facing these trials as well?

We then apply the same way of thinking. In the example of losing a job, it's easy to fall into despair or, on the opposite side, denial. If you loved your job, relished the security of it, or hoped to be there the rest of your life, losing it can really feel like a death. In a way, it is. So, you call it what it is, a death of safety, a death of being with your friends and colleagues. It's a death because you feel rejected and not as important as you thought. You grieve it and share your hurt with those supporting you.

I HAVE THIS HOPE

But you can also view life's tragedies with hopeful expectation. You let go and say, "Okay, God, I believe this death can be resurrected into something better for me. I trust you." With that, you let go and in time receive the gift of a better job, better health, or better state of mind.

Something good happens to us in this process. When we go through these trials, we almost always grow. Though we don't like to hear it at the time, every challenge and setback in life is an opportunity to become a better version of you. In his book *Principles*, the visionary self-made billionaire Ray Dalio gives this advice as the cornerstone to his success:

Pain + Reflection = Progress[2]

For Dalio, life is all about progress through personal evolution. It's about growth. This growth happens not when we succeed but when we fail, lose, or hit setbacks we didn't expect. This is the key. It's here we have the opportunity to withdraw or curse the darkness, as so many do. Or we can objectively observe it and learn from it. We can call it what it is: a huge disappointment. Whenever we face this kind of pain, we have an opportunity to create a new principle for how to respond if it happens again. Dalio said, "This way, when something bad happens and you have a principle for it, you can simply say, 'Oh it's just another one of those.'"[3] It's the discovery of these kinds of principles, along with the actual stretching that comes in the pain itself, that causes us to progress in any and every area of our lives.

Whether we reflect on it or not, the suffering we face can grow us into deeper, wiser, and more mature people. That's why the in-between of losing a job and finding a new job, for example, should never be hurried. Aside from the fact you may settle for less than the great resurrection job God has for you, you may also miss out on an opportunity to become a resurrected version of you. You may miss the lesson in the loss of the job. In the in-between you may see that it wasn't even the industry you wanted to be in, that you were neglecting your family, or any other number of lessons. Enduring suffering with hope and reflection is good for us.

> THE MORE SUFFERING WE ENDURE, THE MORE READY WE ARE FOR BIGGER ADVENTURES.

Enduring suffering also keeps us from becoming afraid of life. The more suffering we endure, the more ready we are for bigger adventures. Why? Well, because we're not afraid anymore. In his great work *The Hero with a Thousand Faces*, American mythologist Joseph Campbell wrote about the hero's journey.[4] He says nearly every great story and myth throughout human history follows the same pattern. An unlikely character in an ordinary world receives a call to enter a world of adventure. He chooses to go on this journey and will face a number of trials and challenges, meeting friends along the way who will help him. Ultimately the hero will have to face the greatest challenge, typically alone, and it will nearly kill him. If he survives the challenge, he will receive a boon, a great gift, which he can bring back to help the world.

Campbell believed that nearly every great story in history followed something close to this pattern. Even today some of the most successful series, like the *Lord of the Rings*, Harry Potter, and Star Wars, all follow this map. This "hero's journey" resonates with all of us. Why? Because, like the hero, we are all called to adventure. When we face the challenge of a lifetime and encounter the thing that almost kills us, we know there can be a gift found within the struggle. The story of the hero is the story of human existence. When we endure our suffering, we not only receive a boon, a resurrection gift, but we also become less afraid of saying yes to the next adventure, and that's a gift in and of itself.

Believe that in every obstacle or challenge there is the possibility for something better. Learn to trust that, even in the darkest times, God can turn a loss into a real victory. See every obstacle as a temporary opportunity for a permanent gift.

Training

VERSE TO MEDITATE ON

"Unless a kernel of wheat falls to the ground and dies, it remains only a single seed. But if it dies, it produces many seeds." (John 12:24)

QUESTION TO CONSIDER

What was a time in my life when a major loss or setback turned out to be a boon, a gift?

THOUGHT TO INHERIT

Every loss and challenge can be a doorway to a better version of me.

DISCIPLINE TO PRACTICE

Ray Dalio suggests that true growth happens when, after our suffering, we take time to reflect and develop new principles or characteristics. This is a discipline that can lead to rapid personal growth. Most of us can't reflect on our suffering when we're in the midst of it. We are tired and are likely experiencing a flurry of emotions. When we get through them, we typically don't reflect because we want to celebrate or go do something fun. Plus, spending more time thinking about the horrible thing we went through sounds exhausting.

The discipline, then, is to take some time, perhaps with a legal pad, and just think about what happened, write down ways you can handle the situation better if it happens again, and think about some healing that may need to happen. Give yourself an hour or so. Make this a time of prayer and listening to get insight from God. Perhaps go somewhere beautiful and relaxing to take the edge off of reliving the memory. In doing this as a regular practice, you will see a tremendous amount of mental and spiritual growth.

CHAPTER 10

FROM WORRY TO COURAGE

I am convinced that courage is the most important of all the virtues. Because without courage, you cannot practice any other virtue consistently.

—Maya Angelou

THOUGHT TO INHERIT: *Doing intimidating things will give me greater serenity in the long run.*

Fear is one of the great traps of the thought life. Fear is something that happens within the mind and works its way into the fabric of our bodies. It has major consequences in our decisions, our actions, and even our health. Whether you suffer from anxiety, worry, or all-out dread, I believe you can become a braver person and remove the grip of fear on your life. You don't do it by trying harder. You do it through training (acts of courage) and through love (nurturing friendships to give you empathy and help you do the scary things with some company).

SUMMER CAMP

When I was a kid, I went to a summer camp for kids from fourth to sixth grade called Indian Village. They put us in different "tribes," and we slept in teepees, made moccasins, and shot with bows and arrows. I loved it.

One of my favorite attractions was this thing called the blob, a gigantic sack of air about twenty-five feet long and ten feet wide, floating on the lake. It floated on the water just under a twenty-foot platform.

To work the blob, you needed two kids. The first would jump

from the platform and crawl to the end of the blob. There he would nervously wait while a second kid would jump from the platform, forcefully pushing the air from the blob when he landed, launching the other kid high into the air and into the lake. To get a feel for how effective this thing was, the world-record blob launch is fifty-two feet high.

The key was this: the heavier the guy jumping from the platform and the lighter the guy waiting, the higher and farther the waiting kid would go. I could see this clearly as a fifth grader, standing on the sandy shore of the lake, alone, admiring these brave kids and wanting to do it myself. I was a skinny guy, not tall at the time, and I just knew if I did this, some big kid would come right behind me. I'd go much higher and farther than is recommended for a kid my size, and I would have a painful landing.

So I watched and I watched and . . . I didn't go.

The next year came around, and heading back to camp, I knew it would be my last opportunity to go on the blob. Every time I thought about it, I got nervous. One of our camp counselors was super popular. He was a big twentysomething Pacific Islander with sweet native tattoos. He was so cool. He was a lot of fun and nice to all the kids. He was someone who would draw kids out and get them to laugh and have fun. I'll call him Big Mike.

When the lake party came and I was faced with the blob, I did it again: I just stared at the blob, both really scared and really wanting to do it at the same time. Big Mike came up and stood next to me, mirroring me as we stared at the blob together. "You want to do it, don't you?" he said. "But you're scared."

"I'm not scared," I said. "Just . . . concerned."

I don't know if it was because he was so cool and I wanted to impress him, or if he was just persuasive, but somehow Big Mike convinced me to do it. With a slap on the back, he sent me running to the platform. I was still scared, but now I was excited too. Yeah, I probably weighed only seventy to eighty pounds, but so did most of the other kids.

When I got to the top of the platform, it became more real. Twenty feet from the ground looking up doesn't seem very high, but twenty feet from up top looking down can be terrifying. But then I saw it—the terror in the eyes of the kid at the end of the blob, the kid I was going to launch. As he looked up at me, he was second-guessing his decision to do this. Somehow that made my fear go away and I leaped, hoping to launch this kid into oblivion. Man, it was great.

It was great until I scooted to the end of the blob and looked back to see who my launcher would be. You may have guessed. It was the 250-pound Pacific Islander, Big Mike. This was bad. I began to panic. Time slowed down as I screamed, "Mike, no!" And with that, Mike screamed like Maui from the movie *Moana* and leapt cannonball style off the platform.

I went so high I actually heard the wind. My arms and legs were flailing, and I was screaming, not even thinking. Then *smack*. Like a pancake on a griddle, I belly flopped. Pain.

Everything I feared about the blob happened. Everything. I got the worst version of the fat-kid scenario I imagined, I flew much higher than I thought was even possible, and I belly flopped like crazy. But when I got up, how do you think I felt? I was in pain, but I felt alive! I was overjoyed! I was jumping up and down, high-fiving anyone I could find. It was awesome. It was awesome because it was fun, the pain was worth it, and most of all, I overcame my fear. Of course, the rest of the afternoon I kept doing it again and again.

LESSON FROM THE KIDS

Maybe you have a story like that from when you were a kid. You and some friends did something you were kind of afraid of, but afterward you felt alive. There was something about pushing through the fear that gave you heart, a sense that *I can do this*. Kids have these experiences a lot, actually, and I believe it's one of the reasons they are generally happier than adults.

A recent study showed that the average child smiles four hundred times a day, but the average adult smiles only twenty times a day. Though many have speculated what's at the heart of this, I think it's that kids are more fully alive than many adults. Children are always facing new challenges they've never faced before. Their lives are scarier and more painful than adults' lives. Though what they have to do doesn't seem scary to us as adults, certain activities really can be terrifying for kids. Think about it. On an average day, children may have to

- make new friends at school,
- take physical risks, like riding a bike down a steep hill,
- stand up to someone being rude or mean, or
- learn how to use new tools and technology.

In short, children are constantly forced into new adventures with the help of friends, parents, and teachers. When we become adults, these types of things still happen to us, but most of them are not new anymore, so they are less scary. The things that are scary and new, we are no longer forced to do. We get to choose to do them, and it's easier now to simply choose not to do them. We are adults after all.

Because we don't live with our parents, we don't have teachers and mentors, and we don't usually spend hours a day with our best friends, we also no longer have the support system to help us do the fun, uncomfortable things that help us grow. In other words, we are free to stay in the rut, and we often lack the love and support we need to get out.

As adults we have some money now as well as the freedom to simply do what we want. This, too, can keep us from doing scary things. By giving in to our worries we agree to live an adventure-free life. Yes, we yearn for adventure, or at least we think we do, but we don't like all the uncomfortable things that come with it. Join the club. Most of us are there.

AVOIDANCE

Ironically, avoiding scary things doesn't make you a less nervous or anxious person. Of course, it's probably best to avoid situations that you know are dangerous, such as entering dark alleys at night or eating food you think will make you sick. But consistently avoiding things that just scare you will make you more anxious, not less. It brings temporary relief, but it harms you in the long run. It's a form of repressing your emotion. Suffering the pain that comes with adventure doesn't make you more anxious, as you might think. It makes you more relaxed. In other words, avoiding fear makes you more fearful, but facing your fears makes you ultimately more at peace.

Psychologist and author Bill Gaultiere wrote about this in detail in his great work *Your Best Life in Jesus' Easy Yoke*. He said:

When you keep avoiding a situation that you're afraid of or stressed by, it provides momentary relief, but in the end it actually strengthens your fear. Some people will develop panic disorder or embarrassing phobias by not dealing with their fear. But the way to be free of anxiety is to face your fears in Jesus' easy yoke of love.[1]

An extreme example of this is agoraphobics, people who are afraid to leave the house. As they avoid anxious situations, the world shrinks around them until they can't leave the house at all. They experience more anxiety over time, not less, as their fear envelops their lives. But there's great hope. Whatever your anxiety or fear, with a deeper relationship with the Lord and in partnership with a friend or loved one, you can move in the direction of the things that make you nervous. You can get real freedom.

"Do not fear" is the most common command in the Bible.[2] Angels often said it just before God was about to do something great in someone's life. Fear may be the biggest thing that stands between you and greatness. It's something that happens almost entirely in the mind, and we can and must overcome it, because fear, worry, and anxiety are the main things that rob our lives of peace and purpose. I believe that if you can train your mind to do things that stretch you, you'll have less worry and anxiety and find more joy in your life.

MOVING TOWARD FEAR IN COMMUNITY

As adults we are given plenty of opportunities to do scary things; however, rarely are we forced to do them. One such case in my own life was when our pastoral team signed up to do what's called a "ropes course." Ropes courses are essentially obstacle courses built in the sky. They are made of very tall planks I can only assume are modified telephone poles, attached to one another with metal wires, ropes, and various wooden obstacles. The purpose of the course is to be simple but scary, and to get a team to go through the gauntlet as an object lesson about fear.

This particular outing would be the fourth or fifth time I'd done a ropes course, and I was convinced this time I wasn't going to let fear get the best of me. The hardest thing about the course is simply walking across a wooden log from one pole to the next. To help you get ready for it, they put an identical wooden log on the ground only a foot or so high. I decided I would go back and forth on it over and over so that when I got to the top I could move based on muscle memory. It didn't work.

FEAR MAY BE THE BIGGEST THING THAT STANDS BETWEEN YOU AND GREATNESS.

As you climb to the top, you have no rational reason to worry. They overprotect you, giving you elbow pads, knee pads, and a helmet. You have a double harness and rope. There is almost no way you're going to get hurt.

I was climbing to the top, feeling good at first, when the telephone pole started to jiggle with my weight now at a higher point. I could feel and hear the wind once I reached the forty- to-fifty-foot height. That muscle memory I was hoping for completely vanished because I was terrified, but I was still trying to look cool and relaxed for my peers watching below. I did not quickly skip through as I'd hoped. I got through, but it took grit, white knuckling my way through, to finish with my dignity barely intact.

It was hard for all the pastors. All of us struggled this way, and some couldn't finish, all except one—Bill Gaultiere. I was just getting to know Bill at the time. We'd both gone to the same university and had hit it off as friends. He ran the New Hope crisis counseling center and was a Spirit-filled clinical therapist, my kind of guy.

Bill did exactly what I'd hoped to do. He gracefully climbed to the top, walked across the log, scaled the wire ladder, meandered quickly across the two-rope bridge, perched on top of the eight-inch-wide platform, and leapt for the trapeze rope to finish. We all watched openmouthed. It's like it was child's play for Bill. To this day it still blows my mind. I asked him when he was done, "Bill . . . how did you do that?"

"I was just walking to Jesus," he said with a smile on his face.

WALK TO JESUS

He really was just walking to Jesus, I've since come to find out. Bill wasn't always this easygoing in stressful situations. He'd be the first to tell you he has struggled with anxiety for years. But by training himself into the easy rhythms of grace, Bill has become what all of us want to be: a man walking in step with Jesus, a man with a serene mind at peace in the kingdom of God. Bill walks the walk and spends a great deal of time every day in prayer and practicing the spiritual disciplines. This has made all the difference. Bill has since become my mentor for many years.[3]

Bill would also tell you the training was not just his friendship with Jesus; it was his relationships with loving, empathetic people who could come alongside him in his worries and fears. It was this empathy and his "knowing I'm not alone in this," that gave Bill (and can give you) the power to push toward the good things in life, despite the fact that something scary is in the way.

TAKE HEART

Being courageous doesn't mean you're not worried. To have courage means you move in the direction of the scary thing. The word *courage* comes from the French word *coure*, which means "heart." It means something has happened to you, and your heart wins over your head. Even though your mind is screaming, *No! Don't do this!* your heart says, *Yes. We can do this.* That heart doesn't come from beating yourself up, and it certainly doesn't come from trying harder. It comes through meaningful friendships and relationships.

> BEING COURAGEOUS DOESN'T MEAN YOU'RE NOT WORRIED. TO HAVE COURAGE MEANS YOU MOVE IN THE DIRECTION OF THE SCARY THING.

When you think about some of the scariest things you've done in life, you likely were able to do them because you had someone standing by your side. In my story about the blob, I wasn't able to do that scary thing no matter how much I tried when I was alone. It was only after Big Mike came alongside and said, "That's scary isn't it?" that I somehow got the heart to press through and do what was scary.

That's the great mistake so many people make about fear. We typically won't have the courage we need if we go it alone. Courage comes from loving relationships. Even if there are times we are physically alone, we are able to do something brave because we've received the kind of training we need for that moment by having people in our lives who love us and have helped us through other scary times.

This is what John means when he says, "There is no fear in love" (1 John 4:18). We have no fear of punishment when we have deep, empathetic relationships with others and with God. We get what we need to deal with our anxiety, worry, and dread. The deeper those relationships go, the more our fear loses its grip on our hearts. Though fear never totally goes away, doing life in deep, meaningful friendships gives us the power to tip the scales toward action.

Many of our modern hero stories are not good in this respect. There are too many stories that have some Lone Ranger who just wills his way through everything frightening. Rather, the best stories are those where people press through the challenges in some kind of meaningful community. This is one reason the *Lord of the Rings* trilogy has been so popular for almost eighty years. It's a story about a group of imperfect people who go on an adventure together, and in doing so they help one another reach their fullest potential.

If you've been bottling it up, trying to face your anxiety alone, I want you to know you don't have to go it alone. We all have worry, dread, and anxiety, but if we don't bring friends along, our worries and fears will begin to choke us very slowly until we can't breathe. You aren't a burden on others. When you share your fears and worries with others, even if you think they're silly, you nearly always find the other person also receives freedom in sharing their worries and fears with you. In this way, love casts out fear for both people. You are given the freedom to give voice to your fears, and that in turn loosens fear's grip on your soul.

TEMPTED TO WITHDRAW

When something worrisome comes along, the temptation to with-draw is strong. Withdrawing doesn't usually mean you say no outright. Rather, it looks like avoiding or procrastinating through outlets like work, napping, or doing something entertaining like watching TV or playing games. All of these things are harmless on their own, but when they're used to avoid something bigger, they can cause long-term harm. Withdrawing when you feel afraid definitely gives you temporary relief, but in the long run it will strengthen your fear. If you do this enough, you may risk getting caught in the very common trap of avoiding the things you dread, which can lead to chronic anxiety.

Instead, when something worrisome happens, get on the phone with a friend or loved one. The right kind of person is the one who will give you empathy and strength to fight. You're not exactly looking for insight at this point. Instead, you're looking for heart (*coeur*) by giving voice to your feelings of fear and worry and receiving love, kindness, and maybe prayer in return.

It's helpful to label the thing you are worrying about. Just say, even to yourself, exactly how you feel.

- I'm worried about giving this presentation tomorrow.
- I know it's irrational, but I'm worried about being a bridesmaid at my sister's wedding.
- I don't like the way I feel at some of these parties. I feel like I'm not going to know anyone.

There are so many times we have a feeling in our stomach, a sense of dread that asks, *Why did I say yes to this?* We don't want to do something, but we've already committed. The worst thing to do is to beat yourself up by saying, *I shouldn't feel this way.* Rather, recognize that pushing it out of your mind or feeling shame will only make it worse. Instead, say to a friend, "I know it's weird, but I'm feeling worried about x, y, and z." It's amazing how labeling and giving voice to your feelings, owning them and not being embarrassed by them, will very often give you real freedom.

Because God loves us, he will rarely let us simply withdraw from scary things. Instead, he will gently hold our hands as he walks with us toward the challenges of life. In a way this is what faith truly is; it's trusting God in the midst of our challenges and anxieties. If we withdraw, find ourselves trapped, and pray for God to help us, he will put us back on the path of personal progress to become courageous people. In other words, he'll put us face-to-face with that old monster, because he's given us what we need to beat it. You don't have to do everything, and you don't have to do it all at once. Simply start by moving toward more of the little things that worry you, and you'll get more heart.

JONAH

It's like the story of the prophet Jonah. He was told by God to go to Nineveh and proclaim God's judgment over the city. This was a terrifying command.

Here's some context: the Assyrian empire was one of the most brutal, cruel civilizations in history. Depending on how you slice it, the Assyrians were the first and longest-running empire in history, spanning across most of the Middle East for nearly two thousand years. Think about that. They lasted about the same amount of time as from the birth of Christ until now. Much of our knowledge of this civilization has disappeared because when the Assyrians were finally defeated, its conquerors wanted to make sure such evil would never come back again, so they killed every man, woman, and child, destroying the capital city utterly.

Torture, burning or skinning people alive, and putting entire cities to the sword was a regular business for the Assyrians. They were a terrifying menace. Nineveh was the capital city of this empire, and it was there God wanted Jonah to go preach God's judgment against it. Jonah's reply? "Nope."

Instead of going east toward Assyria, Jonah got on a boat from Joppa, in what would be Israel, to head to the farthest western city in the known world at the time, Tarshish. It's in what would today be known as Spain. He simply wanted to get as far away from Nineveh as he could. When Jonah was thrown into the sea and swallowed by a great fish, he prayed and asked for God's help. God heard the cry of Jonah, and the fish vomited him onto the shores of Nineveh. God didn't take him back home to Joppa, but rather to the gates of the scariest place on earth, the place of his calling.

If you withdraw from God's call on your life because it's scary, you might find yourself in your own abyss, the dark belly of a fish, wondering how you got there. If you cry out to God, he will do the most loving thing in the world: he'll vomit you on the shores of your destiny. He'll bring you back to your original calling. He'll take you right back to the thing you were so afraid of all those months or years ago, and he'll help you defeat it.

God never gives up on us. He doesn't call you to Nineveh to be killed. He calls you there because you're finally strong enough to take it on. You are finally equipped to do what he's asked you to do. The trouble is, you'll never truly know it until you do it. So do it.

Keep doing scary things just to keep yourself in the habit of not withdrawing. If you don't have a loving, empathetic friendship, make that your number one priority. You can't do life alone. You can't face every dragon by yourself. You need others to come alongside you and help you fulfill God's purpose in your life.

Training

VERSE TO MEDITATE ON

"Be strong and courageous. Do not be afraid; do not be discouraged, for the LORD your God will be with you wherever you go." (Josh. 1:9)

QUESTIONS TO CONSIDER

What's something in my life that I avoid or withdraw from because it makes me feel anxious or afraid? How can I invite Jesus into it?

THOUGHT TO INHERIT

Doing intimidating things will give me greater serenity in the long run.

DISCIPLINE TO PRACTICE

Eleanor Roosevelt famously said, "Do something every day that scares you."[4] She was offering us a practice to change our posture toward the world. Doing scary things, even if they're silly, will train your will to overcome your emotions. You'll experience an unbelievable euphoria when you get to the other side. If you can think of something that would be fun but a little scary for you, I want to encourage you to try doing it. Here's the kicker though: do it with a friend.

Maybe you want to learn how to surf or try a roller coaster. Invite a good friend to go with you to take surf lessons or try that adrenaline fix. Perhaps you're single and you struggle to meet people of the opposite sex.

Ask a friend to go with you where you can ask a guy or girl for a phone number. The point here isn't about learning to surf or meeting the right person. It's about regularly doing scary things to train your mind to be courageous. You'll also see how much better having a friend by your side will make the experience.

If you're not able to make that happen anytime soon, be ready within the next few days to do a scary thing. When the thing comes along, you'll know. Perhaps it's politely confronting someone or pitching an idea at work. Whatever it is, have the phrase "This is my chance" ready to go. When something like that happens this week, say to yourself, "This is my chance! This is the thing Bobby was writing about," and go for it. You'll be glad you did, and it will train you in the direction of fortitude of heart.

CHAPTER 11

SERENITY

The more tranquil a man becomes,
the greater is his success, his
influence, his power for good.
Calmness of mind is one of the
beautiful jewels of wisdom.

—JAMES ALLEN

THOUGHT TO INHERIT: *I can relax and let go.*

Peace. It's what we want for the world and what we want for ourselves. Peace may seem at first to be passive, but peace is powerful and active. Yet it's not something to be grasped. Jesus said, "Peace I leave with you; my peace I give you. I do not give to you as the world gives. Do not let your hearts be troubled and do not be afraid" (John 14:27). As a believer, you cannot achieve peace. Your role is simply to receive it. Embrace it.

Though many achievers don't know it, much of their unconscious drive is simply to feel serene, tranquil, and peaceful. Many people who are pursuing wealth do so with the hope of working really hard now so that later they can retire, relax, and finally have peace. Yet for many, as the years go by, retirement seems further away because they spend their hard-earned money on things that give temporary relief. So, the hope of a peaceful and secure future continues to elude them.

If you've ever been unable to sleep, your mind reeling, unable to relax, you know the value of peace. If you've ever felt relaxed, safe, and unhurried, you've known the value of serenity. Serenity offers clear vision and peace of mind. People would pay or do almost anything to get it. Ultimately, we all want to live every moment relaxed and at peace.

While peace is at hand for all believers, there are disciplines you can implement in your thinking, as well as rhythms in your daily life, that will give you a deep sense of peace and joy anytime and any place.

PEACEFUL MESSIAH

Have you ever noticed how relaxed our Savior was? The Gospels show us this repeatedly. Dallas Willard frequently used this word to describe Jesus. He was relaxed when he walked through a mob that was trying to kill him (Luke 4:28–30). He was relaxed and unhurried when others were pressuring him to be somewhere sooner (John 11:3–6). He also loved naps! The guy took a nap in a storm while the disciples were totally losing their minds from fear (Matt. 8:24–25)! (Next time your spouse teases you for taking a nap, just tell them you are trying to be more Christlike.) Even before Jesus famously turned over the tables of the money changers in the temple, he took time to braid a whip (John 2:15). And after that he began healing people. Why? Because Jesus was and is relaxed. He's our role model for a relaxed mind.

When we put on the mind of Christ, we also take on his characteristics of peace, tranquility, assurance, and grace. When we have a relaxed mind, we take on more than a good feeling. We have clearer vision because we are able to step back and see what is happening without feeling rattled or impulsive.

Clearer vision makes the relaxed person a better leader. It's been said that the "non-anxious presence" in the room is always the one to lead. In a building with a fire, when everyone is scared or screaming, the calm woman who says in a relaxed but direct way, "Everyone, it's okay. We are going out this door and down the steps. Wait on the curb for the fire department to arrive," is the one everyone will listen to. She is the non-anxious, relaxed leader.

You have every reason to relax because God cares for you, he loves you, and he will get you through whatever you're facing. God cares about the things you're worried about. He cares about your anxiety. I once heard a preacher say, "The Bible doesn't say anything about anxiety." He was very wrong. I was surprised someone who was so gifted a Bible scholar could miss the many times Scripture talks about anxiety and gives us the tools to deal with it.

The Greek word for anxiety is *merimnao*. It means something like, "to be torn into pieces." It's nearly always translated as "anxiety" or "worry," but understanding the literal definition is helpful. When you are thinking about so much and worried constantly, you're pulled in so many directions that it feels like your soul is tearing. Jesus used this word *merimnao* when he said, in the Sermon on the Mount, "Do not worry." Here's the tail end:

Instead of looking at the fashions, walk out into the fields and look at the wildflowers. They never primp or shop, but have you ever seen color and design quite like it? The ten best-dressed men and women in the country look shabby alongside them.

If God gives such attention to the appearance of wildflowers—most of which are never even seen—don't you think he'll attend to you, take pride in you, do his best for you? What I'm trying to do here is to get you to relax, to not be so preoccupied with *getting*, so you can respond to God's *giving*. People who don't know God and the way he works fuss over these things, but you know both God and how he works. Steep your life in God-reality, God-initiative, God-provisions. Don't worry about missing out. You'll find all your everyday human concerns will be met.

Give your entire attention to what God is doing right now, and don't get worked up about what may or may not happen tomorrow. God will help you deal with whatever hard things come up when the time comes. (Matt. 6:28–34 THE MESSAGE)

Jesus was showing us that we worry about so much that God has already taken care of. Though we can't see it, God knows what we need and will help us when we need him. He loves us! God loves birds and he loves his creation, but he loves you most of all. We don't have to spend every day wondering if we are attractive enough, successful enough, or even whether he will meet our needs, because he will.

Peace is already ours. We just have to accept it.

RELINQUISH CONTROL

Accepting peace means laying aside our tendency to control. While exerting control can feel active, it's actually counterproductive. Loving others well means letting go of our desire to control or manipulate how they feel.

In our organizations we make this mistake as well. As employers, pastors, or leaders of various groups, we have a temptation to try to control people rather than inspire them. The best groups and organizations attract self-starters who don't need to be micromanaged. They simply need to be inspired. When we hire people who we discover are not self-motivated, we feel the need to micromanage them. When we can't be around to manage them, we feel nervous. *Will they mess up? Will I get a call in the middle of the night?* This, too, takes away our serenity.

The greatest place where control takes away our peace of mind is when we try to control things that are beyond our grasp. Letting go of these things and entrusting them to God is one of the smartest things we can do to gain peace of mind.

Letting go of outcomes doesn't mean we don't do our best. Instead, it means that once we've done all we can do, we should relax and trust the plan and the process. Even more, we should trust God. If something goes wrong or something unexpected happens, it's okay. The world will go on. We give our outcomes to God. We do our best and forget the rest.

DROP THE PERFECTIONISM

Perfectionism is another enemy of peace. I love excellence. I do my best to excel in every aspect of my ministry, music, and media. But if I'm up all night losing my mind over some imperfection, I will cause our whole team to be locked down in operational anxiety. Furthermore, I will simply not be a good friend, father, or husband. Things aren't ever going to be perfect, and the need for perfection is a control issue.

Perfectionism leads to anger toward people who have to do life with us. Your kids and spouse will never be perfect. Your job will never be perfect. Your church, school, and government will never be perfect. Instead of demanding perfection from others, seek excellence. Work hard. Hand over the outcomes to God. And try to have a little more fun while you're at it.

In his great book *Happiness Is a Serious Problem*, Dennis Prager tells the story of visiting a beautiful old cathedral with a friend. Prager observed an ancient tile mosaic on the ceiling and said to his friend, "Wow, isn't that beautiful?" His friend replied, "Yes . . . but . . . it's missing a tile." He just kept staring at it, bothered. His friend struggled to enjoy the work of art because it was imperfect.[1]

INSTEAD OF DEMANDING PERFECTION FROM OTHERS, SEEK EXCELLENCE. WORK HARD. HAND OVER THE OUTCOMES TO GOD.

Prager says we do this in life. He uses the example of another friend who is bald. His friend said, "I'm often unhappy because all I see is men with hair." All of us are tempted to do this. When Hannah and I were trying for our first child, she wasn't able to get pregnant as quickly as we hoped. It took almost a year. During that time, as we started worrying about whether we could even get pregnant, all Hannah could see were pregnant women everywhere. It's the human condition.

When we want a car we can't afford, we see that car everywhere. We think, *If I just had this one thing, my life would be perfect.* The catch is, of course, there will always be a missing tile. If you could actually put that tile in its right place, another would appear out of place somewhere else in the mosaic. It is far better to be at peace with the fact that life will never be perfect. It will always be full of unfinished symphonies. Let go of the need for everything to be perfect in your life, and let go of your need to control. You'll be glad you did.

SERENITY PRAYER

You can see these themes in the Serenity Prayer commonly taught in twelve-step programs. This prayer is pulled from the larger prayer written by the great twentieth-century theologian Reinhold Niebuhr. The one you may be used to looks like this:

> *God, grant me the serenity to accept the things I cannot change,*
> *Courage to change the things I can,*
> *And wisdom to know the difference.*

But the better one, the original, the one that really can lead to great serenity in the kingdom of God looks like this:

> *God, give me grace to accept with serenity*
> *the things that cannot be changed,*
> *Courage to change the things*
> *which should be changed,*
> *and the Wisdom to distinguish*
> *the one from the other.*
> *Living one day at a time,*
> *Enjoying one moment at a time,*
> *Accepting hardship as a pathway to peace,*
> *Taking, as Jesus did,*
> *This sinful world as it is,*
> *Not as I would have it,*
> *Trusting that You will make all things right,*
> *If I surrender to Your will,*
> *So that I may be reasonably happy in this life,*
> *And supremely happy with You forever in the next, Amen.*[2]

In this prayer, Niebuhr is asking the Lord to help him abandon outcomes. He's letting go of the fact that the world is not altogether good, not always the way it should be. He's at peace with the sin of the world, not because sin is okay, but because he believes fervently that God is working to undo it. It doesn't need to take away his peace of mind. He's at peace with the hardship of life. He's relaxed about the fact that life should be lived one day at a time. And of course, at the foundation of it all, he doesn't need to worry about death. He knows death is simply a doorway to greater life for those who put their trust in Jesus Christ.

God does not want us to have anxious minds. He wants us to work hard for the kingdom but also to sleep well at night, knowing he has everything under control. Most of our feelings of control are really an illusion. Letting go of that illusion can be painful, but in the end it will give you a greater sense of peace.

Of course, if having a serene mind were so easy, everyone would have one. Here are some practical ways to help make your life more serene.

Be Present

I was out to dinner with my wife, Hannah, recently, enjoying a nice quiet evening. When Hannah left the table to use the restroom, I grabbed my cell phone reflexively. I hadn't missed a call. I didn't need to read my emails. I didn't have a reason to glance at the phone. It was just a bad habit. This brief moment of self-realization caused me to look around the restaurant. Many people were on their cell phones, even the ones who weren't alone.

There's nothing wrong with cell phones. However, these tools tend to become tyrants if we let them. We can end up serving them instead of living fully in the moment. But overattachment to our phones is just one way to disrupt our tranquility. We must avoid fixating on moments outside the one we're in. With our thoughts fixed on tomorrow—what we'll do and what we need to do before we get there—we can become anxious. When our thoughts dwell on yesterday—what we could have done better—we easily slip into discomfort and lack of peace.

Instead, resolve to be where you are. Be present with the people you're with. If you have a moment to yourself, keep it empty. Just sit and enjoy a moment of tranquility. Develop this as a habit and serenity will become a default mentality.

Statio

There's an ancient Christian discipline called *statio*, meaning "an intentional pause." I find that this practice gives me grounding and focus. I practice it by arriving at my destinations early to think and pray. Say, for example, that I have an important meeting. I'll plan to get there early. If I run into an unforeseeable delay, like traffic, I have a greater buffer on my arrival time. But if it's smooth sailing and I actually do arrive early, I take a moment to quiet my mind, take deep breaths, and open my spiritual ears to the voice of the Holy Spirit. Sometimes I sit in the car and play worship music. The point is to pause in the Spirit.

Try this and see the results. It's a great way to be fully present—with the kingdom of God within you. People will notice. You will be the non-anxious presence in the room, and you'll bring a greater sense of peace to the table.

Don't Hurry

Removing hurry from your life is one of the quickest ways you can bring relief to your troubled mind. Hurry is a practice of self-importance, believing things should happen on *your* schedule. It's a way of subverting God's timing by trying to take control of your future. You can't be relaxed and hurried at the same time. You can't be loving and hurried at the same time. If you want to walk with God, stop running. We must walk with God at a walking pace.

Saint Vincent de Paul said, "The one who hurries delays the things of God."[3] This theme is very strong within Scripture. The most glaring example is when Abraham and Sarah try to hurry God's plan by having Abraham sleep with his servant girl, Hagar. Here you see that not only was God's plan delayed, but great hardship and family brokenness resulted as well. When you let go of hurry, you stop needing to chase your blessing. Instead, you let the blessing come to you.

Be Honest, Always

A recent study showed that, on average, when meeting for the first time, people typically lie *three times* in a ten-minute conversation. These lies are not usually insidious but good-natured in their intent. For example, when one admits to having a flaw, often the other person will confess to having that flaw as well, even though it's actually nonexistent, just to be friendly. Or sometimes when one person says they like a certain thing, the other person will say they like that thing too. Such lies are described by sociologists as a "social lubricant" that helps people find common ground.

If you look deeper, however, this kind of lying is really rooted in the need to fit in, to be liked, and to find a way to get closer to another person. In other words, we most often lie not to get out of trouble (though we do that too) but to get into people's good graces, to get them to let us in, or to help keep them from feeling uncomfortable around us. Sometimes we are lying to be polite.

However, this disingenuous behavior is an offense against

personal serenity. We use up our mental bandwidth trying to juggle the many exaggerations, half-truths, and flat-out lies. Far better to just be honest—all the time. There's too much to remember when you lie.

My philosophy of being awkwardly honest has helped me be less anxious. I often will be so honest it's funny—as in, people laugh. That works as a social lubricant as well. I find that either not saying anything and listening or being totally honest but still totally nice and sincere goes a long way in growing friendships. Why? Because people find authenticity refreshing. They know they can have an honest relationship with you. In other words, they feel safe and serene.

"PEACE I LEAVE WITH YOU"

Ultimately you don't need more money, a vacation, or a stiff drink to have a serene and relaxed mind. You can have it by getting in sync with Jesus' easy rhythms of grace. Let go of your grip on the future or on people. Though it's good to work hard and give it your all, let go of outcomes. Give them to the Lord in prayer. Be at peace with the fact that the world is fallen and imperfect. God's already doing something to change that too. He cares for you.

BE AT PEACE WITH THE FACT THAT THE WORLD IS FALLEN AND IMPERFECT. GOD'S ALREADY DOING SOMETHING TO CHANGE THAT.

So relax, have a peaceful, serene mind, and you'll experience blessing, opportunity, and vision for your life. You'll have the very thing everyone wants so desperately.

VERSE TO MEDITATE ON

"Peace I leave with you; my peace I give you. I do not
give to you as the world gives. Do not let your hearts
be troubled and do not be afraid." (John 14:27)

QUESTIONS TO CONSIDER

In what ways do I struggle with control or perfectionism?
How difficult would it be for me to let go?

THOUGHT TO INHERIT

I can relax and let go.

DISCIPLINE TO PRACTICE

There's an ancient Christian practice called the Breath Prayer. It's a little
weird, but if you can get past that and simply do this in private, it can be
a great benefit. We don't speak Greek or Hebrew, but in both languages
the word for "Holy Spirit" can also be translated "holy breath." Because
of this, monks and other believers would practice breath prayers—that
is, praying deliberately as they inhale and exhale.

The most common way to do this is to take a Bible verse, say the first
half as you inhale (that's the weird-sounding part), hold the breath for
just a second, and then exhale the second part. In this way the scripture
is actually getting into your body. So, as you suck in air you might whis-
per, "The Lord is my shepherd." Hold that for just a half second. Then
exhale, "I shall not want." Just keep repeating this for any amount of
time. This type of meditating on Scripture is a great practice, especially
for relaxing.

A Shalom Prayer

The following Shalom Prayer can help us face fears. It's inspired by Jesus' words in John 14. The goal is to be present to God, his Word and Spirit, as we breathe the words in and out. Use the Breath Prayer technique mentioned above as you pray each line.

- Peace of Christ . . . Not of this world
- Kingdom of God . . . Not of this world
- Fullness of God . . . Not of this world
- Wholeness and health . . . Not of this world
- Shalom . . . Not of this world

Rest in God's loving presence. Then watch and pray with Jesus, calling to mind something you're worried about or afraid of. Or you can intercede for a loved one you're concerned about.

Then return to the Shalom Prayer as a way of taking hold of the hand of mercy that reaches down from the heavens—now and in the time of trial.[4]

CHAPTER 12

OUR GREATEST NEED

*Our greatest fear should not be of
failure, but succeeding at something
that doesn't really matter.*

—D. L. MOODY

THOUGHT TO INHERIT: *Bonding is my greatest need. There are people in my life who love me and want to know me better.*

I never fully understood God's love for me until I became a father. After our first child, Haven, was born, I went through a lot of personal change. I was at home more because we couldn't leave without a babysitter. We had to buy a lot of diapers we couldn't really afford. Also, I wasn't sleeping. But it was all worth it. I loved this child more than is possible to explain.

When she was only a few weeks old, I was holding her in my arms, looking at this little human, and she gave me a huge gummy smile. I thought to myself, *I would do anything for you!* She was bonding with me, and I was bonding with her. I had many more of these types of experiences with her and with my son, Cohen. This is the most important thing a human being can experience: bonding with another person.

When a baby is born, he comes out of the womb, a very warm comforting place, and enters a cold, sterile, scary environment. He comes out screaming and crying, but over the next few months, he makes eye contact with his mother, smiles, and is fed, nourished, and cared for. In this way the baby internalizes the love of the mother so that when the mother is away from him, he still has a deep, unconscious love nourishing him. As the baby develops, he will internalize the love of others—his father, siblings, and friends—and those bonding relationships will help him enjoy a life of meaning and fulfillment because his deepest need is met.

Unfortunately, it's very common for babies and children to not get enough of this kind of bonding, and they will have to do hard work as adults to believe they matter and are worthy of love and belonging. The temptation will be to find distractions in other things that bring temporary relief from the emotional isolation they sometimes feel. That's why things like success without bonding can be so dangerous. On the outside, things are great. We have lots of friends, our marriage is okay, we're doing well vocationally or financially, but on the inside we are numb, unfulfilled, and we are lacking something. This something is almost always a deep connection with family, friends, and God.

Our shame and lack of bonding, believing we are not lovable, can lead to total emptiness. The good news is, the opposite is also true. When we are bonding with friends, family, and God, we come alive. That's why our relationships need to be the most important things in our lives.

Think about a time when you were with a dear friend, sharing your dreams and fears, joys and failures, and received compassion, celebration, or maybe a much-needed hug. Time likely flew by as you were having your deepest need met. Or think of the opposite, a time when you were with someone you *needed* to bond with, maybe your spouse or a parent, but the conversation was only about the weather and other surface stuff. It probably felt boring or even exhausting as unconsciously you were reminded that you were lacking what you truly needed: deep connection.

SATAN'S FIRST ATTACK

God has created us not to live in emotional isolation; he's created us to need one another. Because of this, Satan's first attack is almost always on our relationships. He loves to split people up, split churches, families, friendships, and countries, before he attacks them in other ways. When we are deeply bonded and empathize with one another, we are galvanized mentally and spiritually to endure suffering to victory. But when we are isolated emotionally, we lose the thing we need most to endure—love.

The main way Satan attacks is through deception. The kingdom of darkness is founded on deception. He will tell you lies about yourself:

- The angry part of you is unlovable. Don't feel or share your anger.
- The addicted part of you is unlovable. Fight the addiction on your own.
- The unsuccessful part of you is unlovable. Lie about your status so others will respect you.

On and on he goes to get you hiding your heart from people who need to see you and love you.

Satan wants to create division by spreading fear through deception as well. Like the fox in *Chicken Little* who spreads lies in the henhouse that the "sky is falling," Satan does this to bonded groups of people to get them to stop trusting one another, trust being the main ingredient needed for bonding. In separating loved ones emotionally, he is able to pick them off one by one. Through fear of sickness, poor finances, dangerous outsiders, and so on, he gets into the hearts of people, which leads to brittleness of the heart and eventually separation. Don't let this happen in your family, church, or country. Win the mind game through gentleness, patience, and listening. Draw out from others their feelings and thoughts and always make your relationships the most important thing.

THE BODY OF CHRIST

Deep connection with people is one of the greatest ways God is able to reveal himself to us. Most of the time when someone comes to faith in Christ it's not because they read something or even had some one-on-one encounter with God. It was usually through a friend or loved one who prayed for them, encouraged them, or showed them a better way. In short, most unchurched people come to faith by bonding with believers.

Believers then continue to grow in their relationship with God through other believers, not just independently with God. Ronald Rolheiser points this out as the difference between a theist (a person who believes in God) and a Christian (a person who believes in Jesus Christ).[1] For the theist, a relationship happens existentially. It's a one-on-one personal relationship with God only, I would say, as a straight line. But for a Christian, the relationship is more than that; it's also a straight line with and through other believers, a triangle.

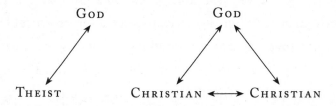

When my wife and I were in premarital counseling, the Christian marriage and family therapist explained this triangle as fundamental to a Christian marriage. When the two move closer to God, they also move closer to each other.

What he didn't point out, however, is that when two Christians move closer to each other, whether they are married or in a friend-ship, they also grow closer to God. Imagining both people are on a track to God, physics would suggest the tension between the two people would also pull them closer to God. Imagine, for example, the two people in this model were holding a tug-of-war rope but they were still on a track that goes toward God. As they pull on the rope to draw closer to each other, the increased tension would also draw them up toward God.

This really happens. I'm convinced one of the main reasons people are struggling in their relationship with God is because they aren't doing the hard work of bonding with friends and family. I know from personal experience. Have you ever tried to go on retreat, have a quiet time, or listen to worship music in your car with the hopes of having some kind of touch from Heaven, only to be disappointed? Maybe, like David, you said in your heart, *Lord, where are you?* It's possible the Lord is saying, *I'm in the church.*

"The church" here doesn't mean a building or an event. The church is the real presence of Christ on earth in people. We call this "the incarnation": when God became a man in Jesus Christ and then, after the ascension, sent the Holy Spirit to dwell in the bodies of believers. In short, as Rolheiser says, "We put skin on God."[2] It's not that I'm a god or you're a god, but God dwells in the bodies of believers.

This has very real and very cool ramifications when you think about what God is doing through his Holy Spirit in the church.

When another believer prays with you, Jesus is praying with you through that person. When you are grieving and another believer weeps with you, Jesus himself is weeping with you through that person's body.[3]

There once was a boy who was crying in bed because of a thunderstorm outside. When his dad came to comfort him, he said to the boy, "Don't worry, son. God will keep you safe and comfort you." The boy put his hands on his father's cheeks and said, "I need a God with some skin on him!" We all need this. We need to experience God both individually and through other believers. We need a God with some skin on him. We need to bond deeply with others to truly enjoy life with less anxiety and loneliness.

YOU ARE LOVABLE

It is vital that we believe we are lovable. But it is also important to reach out to others for compassion, empathy, and even healthy fun. You need relationship with others and they need it from you. The process of internalizing love begins with the mother but continues through life as an ongoing journey of joy. We are nourished by love and suffocate without it.

As much as success is a great part of our spiritual lives, when we obsess over the next big thing, this may be a deeper cry for bonding. When we crave drugs, alcohol, shopping, or gambling, this is really the craving for love. When we harm ourselves to "feel again," we're driven by the need to be seen deeply and loved deeply.

Love is the heart of the gospel. It's the greatest commandment on which all the Bible and commandments therein hinge:

He answered, "Love the Lord your God with all your heart and with all your soul and with all your strength and with all your mind"; and "Love your neighbor as yourself."

. . . Jesus replied, "Do this and you will live." (Luke 10:27–28)

When we love God *and* love our neighbor, we come alive!

WHAT DOES MY NEIGHBOR REALLY NEED?

This is why we must be careful about defining love by what we do to, or for, other people. Love is more than that; it's not merely a verb. Love is caring for the human good. At the deepest level, love is experienced as deep bonding and empathy with others. Your neighbor really needs your heart.

WE ARE NOURISHED BY LOVE AND SUFFOCATE WITHOUT IT.

When we were heavily involved with a homeless shelter in Santa Ana called Isaiah House, I learned the real need of the homeless was greater than food and shelter. When new volunteers came to serve coffee and pancakes, they wanted to do only that: cook, clean, and serve. Though their intentions were commendable, we had to teach that a deeper need should be met. "Go out there and listen, comfort, and pray with these people," we would train volunteers. "Don't just serve them food. Sit down and eat with them. Listen to them. Hear their stories."

The mostly women and children in this shelter were so vulnerable. Many of them had been through severe trauma. They'd been ignored or harassed by people in the city, and they felt hopeless and desperate. They needed food and shelter, but they also needed a friend. They needed bonding, empathy, compassion, and care.

Everyone needs these things, though, not just the poor. Bonding is the greatest human need. We die spiritually without love.

BE VULNERABLE

Being vulnerable is the key to unlocking any relationship in which further bonding is needed. It's also extremely hard to do if you're not used to it. Vulnerability basically means you're willing to let your guard down and show the stuff in your life you think is unlovable or not respectable to others. In doing so, you allow yourself to be seen with the hope that you'll still be accepted, even loved. Most of us have been vulnerable in the past, typically as children or teenagers, and we didn't receive the empathy, understanding, or compassion we hoped for. We were teased, rejected, or embarrassed, and we decided, *Well, that sucked. I'm never doing that again.*

Unfortunately, when we close off the parts of our lives we are embarrassed about, we also cut ourselves off from the deepest love we can experience. It's like we are partly loved but not totally loved. This only leads to more emotional isolation, fear, and deadness on the inside.

Vulnerability can happen when we trust someone enough to risk being our truest self with him or her, hoping they will accept us. The more we practice vulnerability with select people, the safer we'll feel and the more risk we'll take to bond with others. This positive feedback loop will grow over time and make us healthier in nearly every aspect of life.

Your vulnerability is a great gift. It says two things. First, "I trust and love you so much that I'm willing to let you know this thing about me that I won't allow others to see. You're special to me." You may be surprised by how the people closest to you, especially your spouse and kids, need this from you. Second, vulnerability says, "I'm not as perfect as I pretend to be or as you think I am. You are safe to be your true self around me." This kind of safety opens up the heart of your loved one to feel safe around you. This is a huge gift.

BE AWARE

To experience deeper bonding, we must be aware of the pain of others. This can be difficult when we are in pain or isolation ourselves. When we have no energy and are completely exhausted, it makes sense that we "just can't help right now." But when we are vulnerable and bonding in deeper relationships, we are free to broaden our sphere of compassion and care with joy.

The word *compassion* literally means "to suffer with." As we bond with suffering people, we bring a great end to the deception and spiritual isolation intended by Satan. We unify, encourage, and help people endure through loving friendships. This broadening of the circle can become life-giving to us and help us realize God's active presence in our lives in such a rich way that we can even love our enemies. Jesus told us that is the true mark of a mature disciple.

BE GENTLE

To that point, as we love people we are always going to have moments of tension, disagreement, and hurt feelings. It's important that we don't hurt one another emotionally when we disagree. By being violent in our speech and posture, or by punishing through things like stonewalling, we make others feel they are not safe around us. They can't make mistakes. Judgment, harshness, and name-calling always drive us into further isolation and deadness.

Be gentle when you're tempted to be harsh. Even when dealing with our enemies or others in debate, we must always be gentle. Dallas Willard said that gentleness is alluring.[4] It's the main way you'll effectively get through to your spouse, kids, friends, and even enemies. You won't get through by winning an argument. You won't get through by getting some third party to agree with you to pile it on. You'll get through by patiently trusting the Lord to do his thing. You'll get through by being kind. As it's been said, "No one ever came to Jesus by losing an argument."

> AS WE BOND WITH SUFFERING PEOPLE, WE BRING A GREAT END TO THE DECEPTION AND SPIRITUAL ISOLATION INTENDED BY SATAN.

Our relationships are the most important things in our lives, and we must handle them with care. Henri Nouwen compared a loving relationship to that of holding a wounded bird that can't fly, gently supporting the bird in cupped hands. If you squeeze too tightly you will crush the poor thing.[5] This is what we do when we are afraid of someone abandoning us or when we try to control the outcomes in our relationships. But we also can't hold the bird too loosely, or it will fall and die. This is what happens when we are careless, aloof, or absent. This can especially happen when we want "freedom," because we haven't yet discovered that true freedom comes from a loving connection with another person.

People need you, and you need people. Life is too harsh to do alone. We are losing many of our thought battles because we are fighting them alone. In isolation we become fragile, worn out, and dead inside. But when, slowly over time, we build abiding, deep relationships with others, we receive life, joy, and freedom.

Training

VERSE TO MEDITATE ON

"What good is it for someone to gain the whole
world, yet forfeit their soul?" (Mark 8:36)

QUESTION TO CONSIDER

What do I want people to say about me at my funeral?

THOUGHT TO INHERIT

Bonding is my greatest need. There are people in my
life who love me and want to know me better.

DISCIPLINE TO PRACTICE

Write down below what you want people to say about you at your funeral. This practice will help you understand what your real values are and help you begin to see when and if you're investing energy and time into things that ultimately mean little to you.

The goal is to live in line with your authentic values, thus feeling happier and more fulfilled. Is there anything you can change today to move your life more in that direction?

ACKNOWLEDGMENTS

I'm so grateful for the opportunity to write *Change Your Thoughts, Change Your World*. There are many writers and thinkers who clearly influenced this work, so much so that it wouldn't exist without them. I think of Dallas Willard, who taught me "a person is a mind with a will," of James Allen, who wrote the great essay *As a Man Thinketh* over a hundred years ago, and I think of Norman Vincent Peale, who is the originator of this book's title. Most of all, I think of his dear friend, my grandpa, Robert H. Schuller, who taught everyone that our dreams should be big enough to fit God in and that our whole world was the result of our thinking.

I want to give a special thank you to Ami McConnell, who helped me write not for a seminary class, but for hurting people. I'm very thankful to Matt Yates and his team for helping me see this idea could be a terrific book. Most of all I'm so thankful for the team at Nelson Books who have worked so hard to get this book into your hands; especially Jenny Baumgartner and Brigitta Nortker.

I'm also very grateful for our whole team at Shepherd's Grove Presbyterian and Hour of Power. Especially Robert Laird and Jon Essen who helped me with the promotion of this work. There's nothing like having a great team you love, enjoy being with, and can trust with the most important things in your life.

Finally, to my family, especially the one this book is dedicated to, my beloved wife and best friend Hannah Schuller. I couldn't think rightly without you. You are loved.

NOTES

CHAPTER 1: YOU ARE WHAT YOU THINK ABOUT

1. Angela Duckworth, *Grit* (London: Vermillion, 2017).
2. James Allen, *As a Man Thinketh* (San Diego: The Book Tree, 1902, 2007), 27.
3. This quote is often attributed to Martin Luther, but most scholars agree it is not something he said.
4. Stacey Lastoe, "The Unexpected Reason Your Dad's Income Matters to You (That Has Nothing to Do with Inheritance)," The Muse, https://www.themuse.com/advice/the-unexpected-reason-your-dads-income-matters-to-you-that-has-nothing-to-do-with-inheritance.

CHAPTER 2: FROM BLAME TO BLESSING

1. Allen, *As a Man Thinketh*, 49.
2. Dr. Gail Matthews, quoted in Mary Morrissey, "The Power of Writing Down Your Goals and Dreams," HuffPost, updated December 6, 2017, https://www.huffingtonpost.com/marymorrissey/the-power-of-writing-down_b_12002348.html.
3. Jaleesa M. Jones, "99-Year Old Woman Graduates from College," *USA Today*, June 8, 2015, https://www.usatoday.com/story/news/nation-now/2015/06/08/99-year-old-woman-graduates-from-college/28701339/.
4. Daniel Fisher, "Meet the African-American Billionaire Businessman Who's Richer than Michael Jordan," *Forbes*, September 29, 2015, https://www.forbes.com/sites/danielfisher/2015/09/29/meet-the-african-american-billionaire-businessman-whos-richer-than-michael-jordan.

5. Nick Vujicic, in a personal interview with the author.

6. Viktor E. Frankl, *Man's Search for Meaning: An Introduction to Logotherapy* (New York: Simon & Schuster, 1984).

7. Bill Gaultiere, "Pray for the Success of Competitors," *Soul Shepherding* (blog), December 3, 2018, https://www.soulshepherding.org/pray-success-competitors/.

CHAPTER 3: YOU ARE FAVORED. YOU HAVE A DESTINY.

1. Dallas Willard, *The Divine Conspiracy: Rediscovering Our Hidden Life in God* (New York: HarperOne, 1998).

2. Associated Press, "One Victim Survives Her 2d Bus Bombing," *New York Times*, July 25, 1995, http://www.nytimes.com/1995/07/25/world/one-victim-survives-her-2d-bus-bombing.html.

3. Chelsea Wald, "How to Be Lucky," *Nautilus*, January 26, 2017, http://nautil.us/issue/44/luck/how-to-be-lucky.

4. Richard Wiseman, "The Luck Factor," http://richardwiseman.com/resources/The_Luck_Factor.pdf, originally published by the *Skeptical Inquirer*, May/June 2003.

5. Wiseman, "The Luck Factor."

6. John Matby, quoted in Wald, "How to Be Lucky."

7. "Paul's Appearance—What Did Paul Look Like?" *International Standard Bible Encyclopedia*, Religion Facts, updated January 25, 2017, http://www.religionfacts.com/library/isbe/pauls-appearance.

8. Maria Goff, *Love Lives Here* (Nashville: B&H, 2017), 13.

CHAPTER 4: SELF-TALK AND SHAME

1. Direct message from Megsehill to the author on Instagram.

2. *The NAS New Testament Greek Lexicon*, s.v. "charis," accessed August 30, 2018, https://www.biblestudytools.com/lexicons/greek/nas/charis.html.

3. Dallas Willard, *The Great Omission: Reclaiming Jesus' Essential Teachings on Discipleship* (New York: HarperOne, 2014).

4. To see the whole prayer, visit our website at www.HourofPower.org.

CHAPTER 5: FEELINGS VERSUS ACTION

1. Mel Robbins, *The 5 Second Rule: Transform Your Life, Work, and Confidence with Everyday Courage* (Dallas: Savio Republic, 2017).

2. Roy F. Baumeister and John Tierney, *Willpower: Rediscovering the Greatest Human Strength* (New York: Penguin, 2012).

3. Ronald Rolheiser, *The Holy Longing: The Search for a Christian Spirituality* (New York: Doubleday, 1999).

CHAPTER 6: BUILDING A VISION FOR YOUR LIFE

1. You will find more tips for this in chapter 12, "Our Greatest Need," on bonding.

CHAPTER 7: REST AND INVEST IN YOU

1. See Charles T. Munger, *Poor Charlie's Almanack: The Wit and Wisdom of Charlie Munger*, ed. Peter D. Kaufman, 3rd ed. (Marceline, MO: Walsworth, 2005).

2. "Shark Tank Stars Mark Cuban and Sara Blakely Tell Us How They Got to Their First $1 Million—And How You Can, Too," *Time Money*, August 14, 2017, http://time.com/money/4892234/mark-cuban-sara -blakely-interview-how-to-get-rich/.

3. Dave Martin, in a personal conversation with the author.

CHAPTER 8: GOD LOVES MY BODY

1. John Ortberg, *Everybody's Normal Till You Get to Know Them* (Grand Rapids, MI: Zondervan, 2014), 33.

2. Sarthak Bal, "A 10,000 km in 100 days! Ultra-marathoner Samir Singh Falls Agonisingly Short," *Hindustan Times*, updated August 9, 2017, www.hindustantimes.com/other-sports/marathon-man-samir-singh-s -near-10-000-km-run-for-faith/story-3S61LG1l9r16EvqKeTFW1.html.

CHAPTER 9: FROM OBSTACLES TO OPPORTUNITY

1. Ryan Holiday, *The Obstacle Is the Way: The Timeless Art of Turning Trials into Triumph* (New York: Penguin, 2014), 1.

2. Ray Dalio, *Principles* (New York: Simon & Schuster, 2017), loc. 2203 of 8213, Kindle.

3. Dalio, *Principles*.

4. Joseph Campbell, *The Hero with a Thousand Faces* (Mumbai: Yogi Impressions, 2017).

CHAPTER 10: FROM WORRY TO COURAGE

1. Bill au Gualtiere, *Your Best Life in Jesus' Easy Yoke: Rhythms of Grace to De-Stress and Live Empowered* (self-pub., Create Space, 2016).
2. Earlier I said that "Honor the Sabbath" is the most common "moral command" in the Bible. The command "Do not fear" is actually more commonly mentioned than "Honor the Sabbath," but it is not specifically considered to be a moral mandate.
3. To learn more about Bill's ministry to pastors and leaders, check out his many articles on soulshepherding.org.
4. Source?

CHAPTER 11: SERENITY

1. Dennis Prager, *Happiness Is a Serious Problem: A Human Nature Repair Manual* (New York: Regan Books, 1999).
2. Source?
3. Vincent de Paul, quoted in Alan Fadling, *An Unhurried Life: Following Jesus' Rhythms of Work and Rest* (Downers Grove, IL: IVP, 2013), 15.
4. Bill Gaultiere, "Face Your Fears," *Soul Shepherding* (blog), accessed December 3, 2018, https://www.soulshepherding.org/2014/07/face-fears/.

CHAPTER 12: OUR GREATEST NEED

1. Ronald Rolheiser, *The Holy Longing: The Search for a Christian Spirituality* (New York: Crown, 2014).
2. Rolheiser, *The Holy Longing*.
3. It's this belief that drove much of the apostle Paul's writings regarding sexual purity. It was like he was saying, "What are you doing with your body?! God lives in there!"
4. Dallas Willard, *The Allure of Gentleness: Defending the Faith in the Manner of Jesus* (New York: HarperOne, 2015).
5. Henri J. M. Nouwen, *Lifesigns: Intimacy, Fecundity, and Ecstasy in Christian Perspective* (New York: Image, 1986).

ABOUT THE AUTHOR

BOBBY SCHULLER is lead pastor at Shepherd's Grove church in Garden Grove, California, and the host and preaching pastor of *Hour of Power with Bobby Schuller,* a television ministry that broadcasts around the world. Bobby graduated from Oral Roberts University in 2003, received his master of divinity degree from Fuller Theological Seminary in 2008, and is an ordained minister in the Reformed Church in America. He resides in Costa Mesa, California, with his wife, Hannah, and their two children, Haven and Cohen.